LIBERATING TEXTS?

LIBERATING TEXTS?

Sacred scriptures in public life

Edited by
SEBASTIAN C. H. KIM
and
JONATHAN DRAPER

First published in Great Britain in 2008

Society for Promoting Christian Knowledge
36 Causton Street
London SW1P 4ST

British Library Cataloguing-in-Publication Data
A catalogue record for this book is available from the British Library

ISBN 978–0–281–05856–3

1 3 5 7 9 10 8 6 4 2

Typeset by Graphicraft Ltd, Hong Kong
Printed in Great Britain by Ashford Colour Press

Produced on paper from sustainable forests

Contents

Contributors

Dan Cohn-Sherbok was born in Denver, Colorado and educated at Williams College and the Hebrew Union College-Jewish Institute of Religion. He received a PhD from the University of Cambridge and an honorary DD from the Hebrew Union College-Jewish Institute of Religion. He is currently Professor of Judaism at the University of Wales (Lampeter). He is the author and editor of over eighty books including *Israel: The History of an Idea*, *The Palestine-Israel Conflict* and *The Politics of Apocalypse: The History and Influence of Christian Zionism*.

Jonathan Draper is Canon Theologian of York Minster. Previously he was Vicar of Putney in south-west London, and taught systematic theology at Ripon College, Cuddesdon, and was a member of the Faculty of Theology at Oxford University. He is the author of *To Love and Serve* (SPCK, 2003). He is married with three children.

David F. Ford began his career in 1976 as a lecturer at the University of Birmingham and he went on to become a senior lecturer; in 1991 he became Regius Professor of Divinity at the University of Cambridge. Professor Ford has had his work widely published in a range of theological and interfaith journals as well as being author and co-author of several books. He is also a co-founder of the Society for Scriptural Reasoning and is currently Acting Director of the Cambridge Interfaith Programme. Professor Ford's interest and expertise lie in the shaping of universities and particularly the fields of religious studies and theology within universities. He is also interested in interfaith dialogue and the relation of faiths to secular cultures, traditions and forces.

Sebastian C. H. Kim is Professor of Theology and Public Life in the Faculty of Education and Theology of York St John University, UK. He is a Fellow of the Royal Asiatic Society and the author of *In Search of Identity: Debates on Religious Conversion in India* (2003). He was formerly Director of the Christianity in Asia Project and taught World Christianity at the Faculty of Divinity of the University of Cambridge. He is founding and current Editor of the *International Journal of Public Theology*.

John Sentamu graduated in law from Makerere University, Kampala, and was an Advocate of the High Court of Uganda. He practised law both at the Bar and at the Bench before he came to the UK in 1974. He read theology at Selwyn College Cambridge where he gained a master's degree and a doctorate. Following his ordination in 1979 he served in various parishes and was appointed Bishop of Stepney in 1996, Bishop of Birmingham in 2002, and Archbishop of York in 2005. He is Primate of England and Metropolitan, a member of the House of Lords and a Privy Counsellor, and the Chancellor of York St John University. He is married to Margaret, and they have two grown-up children, Grace and Geoffrey.

Ataullah Siddiqui is the Director of the Markfield Institute of Higher Education, where he also teaches Islam and Pluralism, and Inter-Faith Relations. He is a Senior Research Fellow at the Islamic Foundation and Visiting Fellow in the Centre for the History of Religious and Political Pluralism, University of Leicester. He is the Vice-Chair of the recently established Christian–Muslim Forum and the President of the Leicester Council of Faiths. He has written a number of publications and has contributed chapters in several books including: '*Believing* and *Belonging* in a Pluralist Society – Exploring Resources in Islamic Traditions' in David A. Hart (ed.), *Multi-Faith Britain* (2002), 'Islam and Christian theology' in *The Modern Theologians*, edited by David Ford (2005). He is also the author of a commissioned report, 'Islam at Universities in England: Meeting the Needs and Investing in the Future' (2007).

Shirley Williams' career began in journalism in the 1950s. In 1964 she was elected as MP for Hitchin and served as a member of Government during the 1960s and 1970s, culminating in her time as Secretary of State for Education and Science between 1967 and 1969 and as Paymaster General between 1976 and 1979. After losing her seat in 1983, Baroness Williams increased her academic commitments, lecturing in Harvard, Cambridge, Princeton and Chicago. Baroness Williams returned to Parliament as a life peer in 1993 and went on to be elected Leader of the Liberal Democrats in the House of Lords between 2001 and 2004. She has written several books. Her most recent work, *God and Caesar: A Personal Reflection on Politics and Religion* (2003), explores the Church and public life in the modern world and how her own faith impacted on her political career.

Frances Young taught theology at the University of Birmingham from 1971, was Professor and Head of Department (1986–95), Dean of Faculty of Arts (1995–97) and Pro-Vice Chancellor (1997–2002). She was ordained as a Methodist minister in 1984. Fully retired since 2005, she continues to contribute to theology, ecumenism and church life. She has been elected a Fellow of the British Academy, and received an OBE for services to theology.

Preface

The medieval walled city of York may seem to some an unlikely setting for cutting-edge discussion of current affairs but the first series of Ebor Lectures, 2006–2007, attracted hundreds of citizens. The resurgence of religion puts a cathedral city like York at the centre of contemporary debates on the role of faith in society. Six contemporary leaders of society – religious, academic and political – were invited to give their perspectives on the relevance of religious texts to public life. Since this ecumenical venture was initiated jointly by York Minster and York St John University, it was fitting that the Archbishop of York, Dr John Sentamu, who is also the first Chancellor of York St John, gave the inaugural lecture. His address and the other five – by Professor David Ford, Dr Ataullah Siddiqui, Professor Frances Young, Professor Dan Cohn-Sherbok and Baroness Shirley Williams – make up the content of this book.

The Ebor Lectures were conceived as a response to the growing need for theology to interact with public issues of contemporary society, and aim to promote public conversation and to contribute to the formation of personal decisions and collective policy-making in economic, political and social spheres. This ongoing series of lectures is organized by York Minster (represented by the Revd Canon Dr Jonathan Draper), York St John University (Professor Sebastian Kim), York Institute for Community Theology (the Revd Richard Andrew), the Order of Carmelites (Fr Wilfrid McGreal) and the Churches Regional Commission (the Revd Liz Carnelley). Kathryn Dunn, Co-ordinator of the Ebor

Lectures completes the Committee. A relevant theme is chosen each year, and the lectures are delivered alternately at York Minster and York St John University between September and June. The combined annual lectures are being published in book form to make them available to a wider audience. Our desire is to use these lectures as an instrument to promote serious thinking and reflection on contemporary issues from the perspective of faith. The lectures relate faith to public concerns including politics, economics, contemporary culture, religion and spirituality, society and globalization. They are also an ecumenical project, which seeks to exchange insights between academic and religious traditions, and to build bridges between churches and other faith groups.

The theme of the 2006–2007 series was 'Liberating texts?'. The first lecture, by the then newly appointed Archbishop of York, Dr John Sentamu, attracted an audience of over eight hundred people, and could not have been a better way in which to have started the series. The final lecture, by Baroness Williams of Crosby (Shirley Williams), attended by almost five hundred people, brought the first series to an impressive and powerful end. None of the lectures attracted fewer than three hundred people which, for a new series of lectures in an age when the lecture is meant to be a 'dead form', is quite an astonishing number. In this first series we were blessed in the quality of the speakers and organizational skills of the staff of York St John University and York Minster, who enabled the series to happen so smoothly, and we would like to take this opportunity of thanking them all.

Acknowledgements

The Editors, together with the Ebor Lectures Committee members, wish to acknowledge those who have contributed to the Ebor Lecture series: the Very Revd Keith Jones, the Chapter and the staff of York Minster; Professor Dianne Willcocks; Professor David Maughan-Brown and the staff of the Faculty of Education and Theology at York St John University; Fr Tony Lester of the Order of Carmelites; and the Revd Stephen Burgess of the Methodist Church. The conduct of the lectures was carried out by Kathryn Dunn, Ebor Lectures Co-ordinator, whose efforts made the series successful, and others who have helped in various ways. In particular, we wish to acknowledge Alex Carberry of York Minster and Sian Henderson of York Institute for Community Theology for their contributions. For the publication of the series, we wish to express our appreciation to Rebecca Mulhearn of SPCK for her insightful suggestions, and to Dr Kirsteen Kim, Dr Esther McIntosh, Pauline Kollontai and Jenny Sykes, who helped process the material for publication.

Introduction

JONATHAN DRAPER AND SEBASTIAN C. H. KIM

Our experience of the world makes it plain that the sacred texts of the Abrahamic faiths (a term often used to speak collectively about Judaism, Christianity and Islam because of the way in which they all look to Abraham as a part of their founding story) are not always experienced as liberating. Indeed the interpretation of those texts and their application to the contexts and problems of the contemporary world are often seen to be a part of the problems of the world, especially of the Middle East, rather than a part of the solution. Claims arising from these texts – claims to land and resources – based on assertions of exclusive, eternal and inerrant versions of truth, have had, and continue to have, profound consequences. Understanding these texts and their use seems an important matter of public life on which the Abrahamic faiths should be asked to reflect in publicly accountable ways – *Liberating Texts? Sacred Scriptures in Public Life* is an attempt to do just this.

Archbishop Sentamu begins this process in an essay entitled 'Uncovering the purposes of God'. He suggests that uncovering God's purposes is a key to the understanding and use of Christian sacred texts and, importantly, to preventing their misuse. God's purposes can be uncovered, the Archbishop argues, through what he calls 'a threefold approach of trust and worship of a loving God, love of neighbour and caring for creation'. Through our worship, our service of others and our careful stewardship of the world in which we live, we can come to know at least something of God's purposes.

The Archbishop places our human understanding and use of the Bible in that context. He writes:

> There is certainly a need for a reference to and an understanding of the Bible if we are serious about uncovering the purposes of God. However, there are serious issues about interpretation and a careful handling of sacred texts which need to be borne in mind if we are to avoid the pitfalls of literalism on one hand and pure symbolism on the other.

Archbishop Sentamu steers us towards understanding the purposes of God through the life and ministry of Jesus of Nazareth, as shown and demonstrated through what he sees as the key texts of the New Testament. In examining what he calls the 'Nazareth manifesto' from the Gospel of Luke, chapter 5, and the parable of the sheep and the goats from the Gospel of Matthew, chapter 25, Archbishop Sentamu, in a method which echoes the approach of Ataullah Siddiqui later, looks at the ways in which these biblical texts provide a mandate for social justice and so challenge Christians into both a more profound engagement with the world and a clearer understanding of God's purpose in creation. Through this engagement with the world on the basis of loving one's neighbour, the Christian begins to learn of the nature and purposes of God and so interpret the texts – and her or his life – with integrity and truth.

Professor David Ford, in his essay 'God and our public life: a scriptural wisdom', approaches the texts from a different, even if related, angle, and seeks to use insights from years of engaging in the study of the Bible with scholars from faith traditions other than Christianity, to help that process of being faithful to God and at the same time open to insight, challenge, and above all wisdom, wherever they are to be found. He writes:

> As a Christian I would also ground it [an understanding of where wisdom is to be found] in a biblical understanding of wisdom. The Bible is notably hospitable to traditions of wisdom in the Ancient Near East and in the Hellenistic and Roman civilizations, and does not see God as confining wisdom to believers; there are many instances of wisdom arising outside Israel and the Church. The practice of the early Church and most later traditions was to engage appreciatively as well as critically with thought and practice in their surrounding cultures. And from within their own traditions many Jews, Muslims, Hindus and others would make similar points about how their wisdom has been drawn from many sources.

Bringing the Bible to bear on matters of our public life is, he argues, a natural thing for Christians. How they do that, however, in ways that produce the wisdom that is necessary in public life, is a matter of the utmost importance:

> Christian history has many examples (from slavery and sexism to the Crusades and apartheid) of scripture being applied to public life in ways that have led to injustice, violence and misery. The further vital ingredient is that the interpretation of scripture has to be wise . . . one element in wise interpretation is that it tries to take the reality of the contemporary situation into account.

In trying to discover the necessary biblical wisdom, Professor Ford spends some time looking at what is arguably the most profound of the books of wisdom contained in the

Hebrew Bible, the book of Job. Here he finds the right kind of challenge that can enable Christians and others to bring a critical, engaged and wise faith to bear on the great issues of our day.

Like David Ford, Dr Ataullah Siddiqui's essay 'Text and context: making sense of Islam in the modern world' also looks at wisdom, but wisdom as a new reading of the text, as Muslims and the West seek to understand and live alongside one another in a context where their relationship needs healing. Looking at what he describes as the 'five phases of understanding Islam and the modern world', and describing three tendencies in approaching Islam from within, Dr Siddiqui argues that searching out and understanding the human condition is a task laid not only on Muslims, but on Muslims in co-operation with everyone else.[1]

> What the Qur'an demands from us is not simply a relationship with God but a deeper understanding of human conditions today, and it encourages us to establish a deeper relationship with fellow human beings marked by dignity and trust . . . In this qur'anic vision of unity and diversity, the human task is to find a way to handle differences. In a society matters should be discussed, debated and a consensus should emerge, and no force should be allowed to countenance aggression and violence (22:39–40). In all these processes Muslims are bound by their belief to co-operate with all – Muslims or not – in securing peace and justice.

Dr Siddiqui's essay seeks to bring an urgency to the need for Muslims to remember the spirit of the text as well as the letter, and to move away from a literalist interpretation of the text. In this way not only can Muslims avoid many present dangers in their relationship to the West, but can also continue to make a valued contribution to understanding and addressing the needs of our world.

Professor Frances Young brings her remarkable breadth of knowledge of both the history and thought of the early Church and of the interpretation of scripture to bear in her essay 'Sacred text and the transcendence of tradition: the Bible in a pluralist society'. Setting her thoughts firmly in the reality of living in a pluralist society, Frances Young explores the nature of sacred texts and how they function in different religious traditions, but also how they point beyond themselves and are thus capable of transcending their traditions of interpretation. As Professor Young writes:

> Each religious community has the potential to discover its own place in the rainbow society of pluralism if it becomes more responsive to its own sacred texts. So sacred texts will prove to have a crucial role in a pluralist society, which is far removed from the assumption that they are just competing and incompatible claims to truth. If allowed to, they can challenge and transform the outlook of their own adherents, so as to make them better citizens of a pluralist world. Furthermore, we can find within the various sacred texts common insights into the human condition, which can contribute to those values which permit a pluralist society to function.

Echoing the kind of approach taken by Professor Ford, Professor Young argues that we need to recognize that our sacred texts, which could push religious communities into ghettos of mutual isolation, might in fact become 'the greatest resource for mutual engagement and a discovery of common values which could contribute to the proper pluralism of the public realm'. Taking their sacred texts seriously could make religious people a force for good in a deeply divided world.

This would not adequately describe the contribution of Rabbi Professor Dan Cohn-Sherbok in his essay entitled 'The

Bible and the Middle East'. In this essay Professor Cohn-Sherbok looks at the ways in which particular understandings of the Bible can lead – and have led – to disastrous political and humanitarian problems in Israel and the Middle East. He cites the long history of Christian interpretation which actively looks for a cataclysmic end to the world based on both the Second Coming of Christ and certain passages of the Hebrew Bible. He shows how this has influenced – and continues to influence – US policies towards and involvement in the Middle East. He also explores the use of scripture by ultra-Orthodox Jewish Zionists, and how they see the Six-Day War as the beginning of the Messianic Age. Professor Cohn-Sherbok also shows the ways in which these two groups – conservative Christian and ultra-orthodox Jewish – have sometimes even worked together to further the Zionist cause.

The challenging conclusion that Professor Cohn-Sherbok reaches in all this is that

> it would be far better to set aside the quest to draw inspiration from the Bible to solve the problems of the Middle East. The example of the Christian Zionists and of Orthodox extremists illustrates the dangers of the selective use of biblical texts. Instead of providing a bridge between Jews and Muslims, the Bible has become an obstacle to peace.

He would have us 'take leave of the Bible': 'Let us take leave of biblical prophecy in attempting to solve the problems that beset Arabs and Jews. Scripture is a hindrance. It is a snare and a delusion.' In this case our sacred texts are a part of the problem and not a part of the solution.

Looking at potential solutions to some of the most distressing and difficult problems in our world is also the theme of the final essay by Shirley Williams, Baroness Williams of

Crosby, called 'Religious traditions in the context of a liberal democracy'. Baroness Williams sets out her thinking in the contextual reality of the pluralist nature of the UK as it has developed over the course of her lifetime. She notes how different a country England is today in comparison with when she was first involved in politics as a young woman in the 1950s. And in the light of that plural reality, and what Baroness Williams describes as 'the remarkable development of what one might call the philosophy of human rights, both nationally and internationally', she examines how, when and to what extent 'the international community has the duty to intervene in cases where states abuse their own citizens'. Using the concept of the 'just war' and the moral obligation generally enjoined on followers of the Abrahamic religions to 'welcome the stranger in our midst and to care for him or her as the Samaritan did in the biblical parable', Shirley Williams challenges us all, in the liberal democracies and beyond, to rethink our engagement with the world, and to draw on and use the resources of our faith to do so.

In spite of a very diverse set of contributors two major themes emerge from these essays. The first is that sacred texts, by which over 3 billion people – nearly half the world's population – live their lives, really do matter, both for good and for ill. And they matter for every aspect of life on our planet from economics and international relations to culture and climate change: no aspect of life is free from the powerful influence these texts exercise. Taking these texts seriously, then, ought to be a matter of significant priority in academic, political and religious institutions. The essays in this book are all a significant contribution to that task.

The other major theme that emerges from these essays is both to note and to celebrate the pluralism of our society – not only in the UK, but throughout the world. We live cheek by jowl with people of other faiths, cultures and ethnic backgrounds in a way in which few other generations and places have done in human history. Of course, we are aware that many places in many times have been cosmopolitan and diverse. However, modern communications and patterns of migration mean that pluralism is now the routine context for most of the world most of the time. This is and has been a source of genuine tension and sometimes conflict; it has also been seen as an enrichment of human life. The fact of pluralism is, however, inescapable, and is the context not only for understanding our sacred texts, but also for how we learn to use and live by them in ways that make for human flourishing rather than conflict. We are hopeful that this book will make a contribution to that human flourishing.

Note
1 References are to the Qur'an.

1

Uncovering the purposes of God

JOHN SENTAMU

What does it mean to uncover the purposes of God? In legal
terminology disclosure is the process whereby the prosecution and defence exchange their documents before a trial
so that each is aware of what the other is claiming to be the
facts of the case, and the evidence they hope to produce to
support both allegations and denials. Through the documents each side gets an idea of where the other is heading,
what evidence they will be relying upon to persuade the jury
of their case, and what their purposes are. In uncovering
God's purposes both for ourselves and for our society, we
are involved in an act of uncovering purposes which God
has already disclosed to us in creation. In this essay I argue
that God's purposes can be uncovered through a threefold
approach of trust and worship of a loving God, love of
neighbour and caring for creation. God will be God without
humanity. But without God humanity would be naught.

The story is told of a man who lived in an area prone to
the most terrible floods. One night the rains begin to fall
heavily and the residents are urged to evacuate. The local
police come to escort the man away, but he tells them, 'It's
OK, God will take care of me.' The rains continue and the
coastguard comes to take the man away to safety. 'It's all
right,' he says, 'God will take care of me.' Finally the man is

forced up on to his roof as his house is flooded out by the rains, and an army helicopter comes to rescue him but he refuses to board, saying, 'It's OK, God will save me.' The man drowned. And when he got to heaven, he came before God and asked, 'Why didn't you rescue me?' 'I tried to save you,' replied God. 'First I sent the police, then I sent the coast-guard and then I sent the army.'

As this story demonstrates, trusting and worshipping a loving God is easier than we would sometimes make it. God's purposes are here for us if only we care to stop, look and hear. Rather than waiting for God to act on our terms, we need to see what God is already doing in our world and to step out in faith and trust if we are to involve ourselves in his purposes. I invite you to join me in spending some time with people who have uncovered the purposes of God in their lives and in our country's history. Through their trust and worship of a loving God, their love of neighbour and their care for creation they have shown where the purposes of God might be found and where we need to begin if we are to learn from their journey. Having considered how God's purposes have been discovered in the past, I then want to consider a world where God's purposes are discarded, before concluding with a brief reflection on what we as individuals and as a society might do in our attempts to uncover the purposes of God.

There are doubtless those who would look at the title of this essay and suggest that to uncover the purposes of God all should be provided with a Bible, be told to sit in silence and read it, and at the end they will have discovered God's purposes. Well, this will not be my approach, although I do have some sympathy for the starting point of that particular argument. There is certainly a need for a reference to and an understanding of the Bible if we are serious about uncovering the purposes of God. However, there are serious issues about interpretation and a careful handling of sacred texts which need to be borne in mind if we are to avoid the pitfalls of literalism on one hand and pure symbolism on the other.

Perhaps the worst system for handling sacred texts is that favoured by the occasional Bible reader who seeks God's purpose by turning to random verses in the Bible in the hope of revelation or receiving an inspired word. Such a faulty system may well lead to turning up a verse such as Matthew 27.5, which says of Judas, 'throwing down the pieces of silver in the temple, he departed; and he went out and hanged himself', followed by Luke 10.37: 'Go and do likewise.' This is not meant in any way to belittle the sacred texts of faith. Later in this essay I will argue that Jesus' words as recorded in the Gospels are an invaluable guide as to uncovering God's purposes, and that for our evidence of this we need to consider the role played by Christian pioneers of social justice in our country's history. However, we must remain alert to the very real danger of misusing texts or selectively applying texts so that they simply become ways of seeking approval for acts which are truly abhorrent to God. This is a topic I will address more fully towards the end of my essay.

'Your God is too small'

In his 1951 seminal work *Your God Is Too Small*, the author and priest J. B. Phillips described how society had surrendered a vision of an all-powerful creator God for an image of a deity which was variously conceived of as the old man in the sky, the policeman of the conscience or a parental hangover. People no longer believed in the God of the Bible, argued Phillips, because sociologists and others had recategorized faith as being a prehistoric necessity of prehistoric man and woman which has no place in the modern world, where human achievements have rendered any sort of conception of God obsolete. At best God was seen as a fluffy pink duvet who may ease our discomfort, should we find ourselves – through bad luck – lying on a sociological bed of nails and an economic pillow of broken glass.

Fifty years on, the situation described by Phillips has, if anything, become worse rather than better. Is it any wonder then that, for many, the place of faith and religious belief systems in general is now 'widely viewed as the lowest form of knowledge'.[1] Britain is tired of its own culture, and the unbridled consumerism and secularism have led many to assume that human beings alone can make themselves. God has been totally shut out. What we are in danger of developing is a culture that excludes God from public consciousness. No bad thing, some might say. We are now free from the hocus-pocus of religion, and can get on with making our own decisions based on the rationale and reason of the Enlightenment. Yet, I would argue, the relegation of religious thought and of religious motivation to the lowest form of knowledge not only runs the risk of negating the role played by Christian champions of social justice but more importantly risks removing those core and essential values of human worth which are essential in discovering God's purposes. Such an approach also forgets the truth of liturgy, in the words of St Bede, that it 'was the Gospel which conferred nationhood on these islands'. As a society we are in danger of suffering from collective amnesia when it comes to considering the work of those who have uncovered the purposes of God in our history. In particular we seem to have airbrushed from history the motivation of those social pioneers who have been inspired to act by a passionate and vivid faith in the God who caused 'his light to shine in the face of Jesus, giving us the knowledge of his glory' (2 Corinthians 4.6).

Let me begin with a brief but wholly incomplete consideration of some of the causes and changes in society which have been achieved by those seeking to uncover the purposes of God for our world and our nation: the abolition of the slave trade in the British Empire, the repeal of the Contagious Diseases Act, free education for children at primary and secondary school, the introduction of licensing laws for the protection of children, soup kitchens, housing for the homeless, and the improvement of prison conditions. Then there are those organizations and charities founded by Christians, many in the last century alone, which have contributed an incalculable amount: the hospice movement, Amnesty International, Shelter, Save the Children, the Samaritans, Alcoholics Anonymous, the Shaftesbury Society, Jubilee 2000, the YMCA, the trade justice movement, the Children's Society, and National Children's Homes. And lest anyone think that these charities and movements are a part of our distant history, we should remember findings by Shelter that over 100,000 households, including 1 million children nationwide, are living in squalor.[2] So bad are the overcrowded conditions in which some of our children live, that Shelter's research suggests a direct link between these housing conditions and a rise in childhood tuberculosis, coughing and asthmatic wheezing. One million children! How is it that we still have such Dickensian housing conditions and even a resurgence of tuberculosis in the twenty-first century?

While the shortage of decent affordable family housing is a major cause in creating this situation, the breakdown of family life is also a contributing factor. The family is the primary social unit. The well-being of the whole community requires that children, so far as possible, be brought up by their own parents as members of one family, with all the give and take that family life demands. For it is within the family that we first learn what it means to love, to trust and to care for one another. We learn how to forgive, how to overcome and how to grow. These lessons are not optional, and for the fabric of society to remain strong, the state and the laws of the land need to support and encourage families. Shelter is just one of the thousands of British charities that exist today only through the Christian beliefs of those who have founded or established them as organizations. While Christians can in no way claim to have a monopoly in the field of social justice, their contribution has been incalculable. As Nelson Mandela suggests in his autobiography, *Long Walk to Freedom*, 'the Church was as concerned with this world as the next: I saw that virtually all of the achievements of Africans seemed to have come about through the missionary work of the Church.'

Before looking at the work and lives of some of those who have uncovered the purposes of God in Britain over the past decades, I want to consider first part of the biblical mandate which would have inspired those pioneers of social justice.

The biblical mandate

Central to any such mandate is the life of Jesus Christ and his central redeeming work in the purposes of God. His life lived out two thousand years ago has inspired millions of men and women to acts which clearly signpost the purposes of God in society. The path these pioneers have trodden is set out most directly by Jesus in two instances of his recorded life as told in the Gospels. The first is what has become known as the

'Nazareth manifesto', and the second is the parable of the sheep and the goats.

The account of Jesus in the synagogue at Nazareth in Luke's Gospel tells of Jesus unrolling the scrolls of the Jewish scriptures and reading from the prophet Isaiah:

> The Spirit of the Lord is upon me, because he has anointed me to bring good news to the poor. He has sent me to proclaim release to the captives and recovery of sight to the blind, to let the oppressed go free, to proclaim the year of the Lord's favour.   (Luke 4.18–19, NRSV)

This prophecy, Jesus tells his hearers, will be fulfilled in Jesus' own life. His ministry will be one of proclamation, healing and release. The resonance of this proclamation has echoed down through the centuries to men and women who have taken Jesus' words as a blueprint for the purposes of God.

The second instance is the parable of the sheep and the goats (Matthew 25.31–46). Here Jesus talks of the day of judgement where those who receive eternal life are those who have fed the hungry, met the thirst of the parched, clothed the naked, welcomed the stranger, and visited the sick and the imprisoned. The care and provision for others who are in need of physical and spiritual well-being is highlighted as being central to uncovering the purposes of God. Central to both of these is the inordinate worth placed on human life as the pinnacle of God's creation. The lives of the oppressed, the captive, the poor and the sick are the lives which become the centre of Jesus' mission on earth: the lives of the have-nots, the down-and-outs, those who live on the margins of society or have been abandoned by it altogether. It is through interaction with these lives that God's purposes are uncovered. Caring for God's creation requires us to care for one another.

The pioneers

The year 2007 was the bicentenary of the abolition of the slave trade in Britain, and there were numerous programmes and events to celebrate the achievements of William Wilberforce. It is appropriate that in the Church of England's calendar the Gospel reading for commemorating Wilberforce's life is Jesus Christ's 'manifesto' proclaimed in Nazareth. Wilberforce was born in Hull in 1759. Rather than becoming ordained, he was encouraged by John Newton that his faith would find expression through politics. His election as a Member of Parliament at the age of 21 marked the beginning of a parliamentary career during which he fought tirelessly for numerous causes, not least for the abolition of the slave trade. After years of effort and defeats in Parliament, the trade in slaves was made illegal in 1807 when Wilberforce received a standing ovation in the House of Commons in recognition of his campaigning to proclaim release to the captives.

Twenty-one years later, in 1828, Josephine Grey was born in Northumberland and baptized that same year. Aged 24 she married an Anglican priest and as Josephine Butler campaigned on behalf of the hundreds of destitute and poverty-stricken women she had met who had turned to prostitution as the only way out of desperate poverty. From 1869 until 1883 Butler dedicated herself to this work, campaigning for the repeal of the Contagious Diseases Act, which criminalized prostitutes rather than those who paid them. For Butler, uncovering the purposes of God translated into letting the oppressed go free. Almost half a century before Butler was born, another Christian woman of devoted service was beginning a lifetime of service to the imprisoned and the homeless. Elizabeth Fry was a Quaker and an evangelistic preacher of great repute, proclaiming the good news of Jesus Christ in London. The appalling state of prisons and the particular ill treatment of women prisoners led Fry to devote much of her time to the welfare and well-being of prisoners, as well as setting up one of London's first night shelters for the homeless in 1820.

Then there are those wonderful Quaker industrialists, whom I would like to call 'The Trinity of Chocolate': George Cadbury, Joseph Rowntree and Joseph Storrs Fry.[3] George Cadbury's faith was his primary motivation, and the fulfilment of its commandments his overriding objective. He improved the living conditions of thousands, influenced legislation, created models for future industry and became a catalyst for social change. His efforts also saw many come to faith – perhaps his most valuable legacy. His biographer notes that: 'He had only one passion – to leave the world a better place than he found it – and he spent his whole life in its pursuit.'[4] Joseph Rowntree (1836–1925) was both an active Quaker and also a hugely successful businessman. As a young man he took over his father's grocery shop in York, but it was in the confectionary industry that Rowntree was to become a household name. Rowntree's legacy, however, spreads far beyond the popularity today of fruit pastilles and fruit gums. Indeed, Rowntree's most important influence is that of a faith-inspired entrepreneur, a progressive industrial patriarch with a deep social conscience, who had a far-reaching, positive influence upon Victorian England. Today, the values and motivations of Rowntree live on, embodied in the Trusts he established, influencing the world beyond the limits of his lifetime. His biographer described him as 'an adventurer to the end of life, forever peering forward, never content with what had been achieved . . . He heard the echoes from the past, and with them he challenged the future.'[5] The third of the Chocolate Trinity was Joseph Storrs Fry II. Born into a Quaker household, Fry became a third-generation confectioner, inheriting the chairmanship of J. S. Fry and Son, Britain's largest chocolate and cocoa manufacturer. In his lifetime, Fry's accounted for a quarter of the chocolate sold in Britain. The family concern had developed a reputation for innovation, quality and honesty, all hallmarks of Quaker industrial practice which was distinctive during this era. Yet, despite his great wealth, Fry has been largely forgotten by history, and there is little in terms of biographical detail available. What we do know however is that J. S. Fry was undoubtedly a generous man, with the heart of a giver and a desire to serve God. In their own ways, and with varying success, each of the Chocolate Trinity sought to enable those who worked for them by giving dignity and meaning to their work and life and leisure. Their desire to serve God as their motivation was unapologetic and unashamed.

I could carry on with examples of great lives lived in the service of others, examples of men and women who have taken seriously Christ's urging and have through their work reflected God's purposes. In Britain alone in the last century there has been Bruce Kenrick, the first chairman of Shelter and one of its founding fathers; Chad Varah, the London vicar who founded the Samaritans, who now receive 13,000 calls a day; Peter Benenson, the young Christian lawyer who founded Amnesty International; and Dame Cicely Saunders, the founder of the hospice movement, who declared that, without the inspiration of Jesus' teaching and the strength given her by his Spirit, the problems she faced would have overwhelmed her. She was not overwhelmed and her work has spread worldwide, while in Oxford in 1982 the first

British hospice for children was founded by dedicated Anglican nuns.

Of course this selection is far from exhaustive and does not begin to take account of the work of all those Christians beyond these shores who have uncovered the purposes of God in their own countries and the countries of others. The names of Mother Teresa, Martin Luther King Jr and Archbishop Desmond Tutu are familiar to all, while the martyrs of the Church such as Oscar Romero and Janani Luwum show us that following the teachings of Christ in the service of others can be as costly as to demand your life. How far away such figures seem from those Christians ridiculed by the psychologists and sociologists for using their faith as a crutch! Faith is not a crutch to lean on. It is the very act of learning.

In my inauguration sermon as the ninety-seventh Archbishop of York, I said that the Church in England must once again be a beacon by which the people of England can orient themselves in an unknown ocean by offering them the good news of God in Jesus Christ in a way practical and relevant to their daily lives. Having shed an empire and its missionary zeal, has this great nation, and mother of parliamentary democracy, also lost a noble vision for the future? We are getting richer and richer as a nation, but less and less happy. The Church in England must rediscover its self-confidence, and the self-esteem that united and energized the English people those many centuries ago when the disparate fighting groups embraced the gospel.

The Venerable Bede, in his *Ecclesiastical History*, tells not only of how the English were converted, but how that corporate discipleship – the Church – played a major socializing and civilizing role by uniting the English and conferring nationhood on them. The history of the See of York tells a wonderful story of York's part in the conversion and civilization of the English. In 627 Paulinus converts the King of Northumbria, Edwin, and baptizes him on Easter Day. Paulinus is allowed to build a little wooden church, the first church on the site of York Minster. It was not easy country. The Venerable Bede tells us that there were villages in these mountains and forests rarely visited by a Christian minister. The first three archbishops here were driven out because of war and revolution. But the small band of Christians, like a tiny acorn, courageously stood their ground. Aidan, a monk from the monastery in Iona, came to the rescue, and extended the Christian presence in the north of England, which radically transformed the existing social order.

In our own time, this socializing and transforming power of corporate discipleship is illustrated further by three young Christian men at the University of Oxford: Richard Tawney, William Beveridge and William Temple, who were challenged to go to the East End of London to 'find friends among the poor, as well as finding out what poverty is and what can be done about it'. In the East End their consciences were pricked by poverty: visible, audible and smellable. After university, Tawney worked at Toynbee Hall, creating a fraternal community; William Beveridge paved the way for the Welfare State in his report, which for the first time set out to embody the whole spirit of the Christian ethic in an Act of Parliament; and William Temple, as Archbishop of York and then Canterbury, mobilized church support for a more just, equal and fraternal Britain. His book *Christianity and Social Order* (1942) is one of the foundation pillars of the Welfare State. It is very clear, then, that the socializing and transforming power of the gospel, lived out in corporate discipleship, was not only in the early Church, in seventh-century

12

England, but in our own lifetime too – and even more recently in two Church of England publications, *Faith in the City*[6] and *Faithful Cities*.[7]

Vision

These basic precepts to uncovering the purposes of God – trust and worship of a loving God, love of neighbour and caring for creation – are not limited in their application to individual lives and circumstances. I believe it is quite possible for the state to adopt these principles in establishing a vision of what it is to govern. 'The art of government in fact', wrote Archbishop William Temple in 1942, 'is the art of so ordering life that self-interest prompts what justice demands.' This marrying of justice and self-interest is deeply unfashionable in a political scene where parties rush to outdo each other in enticing and beguiling the swing vote of middle England, not with justice but with preference and consumer choice. Temple's description of the art of government rings hollow in our rights-based culture. At times the citizen's motto of 'my God and my right' seems to have been replaced by 'my right and my choice'. Political vision based on values has been replaced by consumerist politics, where choice is king, even when such choice is illusory. The main political parties rarely chase the votes of the marginalized. They take their votes for granted.

In a brilliant essay, '*Imitatio* and Ethics in Judaism and Christianity',[8] Professor Raphael Loewe, formerly Goldsmid Professor of Hebrew at University College London, says:

> The whole concept of human rights is one that is alien to rabbinic jurisprudence . . . all humankind are the reciprocal beneficiaries of the duties, which each individual owes to God . . . It is mercy, loving kindness and reciprocal solidarity,

which binds together, at the level of both individual and group, superior to inferior, advantaged to disadvantaged, man to God and God to man. It prevents either self-discipline or social responsibility from being ignored. It is walking in all God's ways. Deed of mutual charity. It is the cultivation of submissiveness to the divine will, and praying, 'Subdue thou our self-assertive drive, to enslave itself to thee'. For the Torah is a golfing-umbrella, not an infinitely extensible bus shelter.

This freshness of thought may help us to get out of the quagmire of human rights debate. These are the core values of true citizenship. Values which were the building blocks that gave nationhood to this nation through the medicine of the gospel. 'Reinventing the wheel isn't the problem; it is reinventing the flat tyre that is the killer.'[9]

Grace

I am not arguing here that Christians, or Christianity, have a monopoly on social justice. Equally emphatically, I want to reject any notion that Christianity is a faith where redemption can be earned on good works alone. That particular ship sailed long ago and sank without trace, but like the *Titanic* it is often recalled. There is a danger that uncovering God's purposes may begin to be little more than the Church or Christians acting as another branch of the social services. As the parable of the sheep and the goats reminds us, our love for our neighbour is grounded in practical and just action, but it must not end there. Without direction, without a spiritual purpose, such action runs the risk of being little more than a sticking plaster which is peeled away with the occurrence of the next tragedy. A famous modern-day rewriting of the parable goes something like this:

I was hungry and you formed a committee to investigate
my hunger.
I was homeless and you filed a report on my plight;
I was sick and you held a seminar on the situation of the
under-privileged and malnourished;
I was in prison and you set up a prayer group for prisoners
of conscience;
I was naked and you bought Cafédirect and Fairtrade
goods.
You have investigated all aspects of my plight and yet I am
still hungry, homeless, sick, naked and in prison.

The late Mother Teresa of Calcutta visited the University of
Cambridge to deliver a lecture on poverty in August 1976.
The frail figure of this Albanian nun climbed up on to the
platform to rapturous applause. When the clapping had died
down she said:

In the West, one of the greatest problems is loneliness.
People die alone. You have the greatest evidence of poverty.
Poverty of the spirit. It can only be fed by the bread of
heaven: Jesus Christ . . . In India our greatest problem is
togetherness. Diseases are easily shared but hardly any dies
alone. We have the greatest evidence of poverty. Physical
poverty. It can only be fed by the bread of heaven: Jesus
Christ.

For all of these Christian pioneers uncovering the purpose
of God has meant being agents of God's grace, God's movement of change, in places and situations that were graceless.
Uncovering the purposes of God entailed seeing that divine
spark in their neighbour and recognizing the incalculable
worth of each individual human being. It meant seeing
each person as a child of God, whose life is measured not
by financial worth, not by a quality of life, not by potential

success of achievement and not by usefulness to society, but rather by valuing people by virtue of their very existence, and acknowledging God as the source of all life and one another as poor but infinitely valuable reflections of the divine image. The person is primary, not the society: the state exists for the citizen, not the citizen for the state.

So at its heart uncovering the purposes of God requires of us as an essential prerequisite to see in one another that image of God himself. Until we can learn to see God in our neighbour, in our enemies and in those we pass by, we will be blind to uncovering God's purposes for ourselves and for our nation.

Change

Once we have uncovered the purposes of God, these can prove to be a powerful catalyst for change in the lives of our neighbours and our country, not least in the laws which govern us. In his 1979 book, *The Discipline of Law*, Lord Denning wrote:

> The principles of law laid down by judges in the nineteenth century – however suited to social conditions of that time – are not suited to the social necessities of the twentieth century. They should be moulded and shaped to meet the opinions of today. But that moulding and shaping cannot be left to Parliament alone. Only too often it is swayed by the political views of the party in power without reference to any moral basis.[10]

In September 2006, Billy Dunlop pleaded guilty to the murder of Julie Hogg, 22, a pizza delivery girl, on 16 November 1989. Mr Dunlop made legal history as the first man to be convicted after the end of the 'double-jeopardy' rule, having previously been found not guilty on two occasions. Although the change to the law came about with the Criminal Justice Act of 2003, the recommendation to bring an end to the injustice of the double-jeopardy rule was made by the Stephen Lawrence inquiry, which was published in 1999. The inquiry recommended that 'consideration should be given to the Court of Appeal being given power to permit prosecution after acquittal where fresh and viable evidence is presented'. The inquiry was committed to truth and justice, and in light of DNA developments believed that it would be wrong for the guilty to go free, just as much as it would be wrong for the innocent to be convicted. The purposes of God can be uncovered in the midst of the deepest of tragedies and the most blatant of injustices. Nowhere is God's will absent or his purposes unfathomable. One hopes that compelling evidence will come to light so that the killers of Stephen Lawrence will be brought to trial.

A world without God's purposes

There is, of course, another path open to each of us, and that is to ignore the purposes of God and instead to recreate God in our own image. For although each of us, as Augustine noted, retains a 'God-shaped hole' within our being, this hole can be filled by other means. Our capacity to worship is transferred so that, instead of worshipping God, we worship the demons of materialism, celebrity or wealth. You only need to go to a football match or a rock concert to see that people's capacity to worship remains very much intact. However, a world where God's purposes are ignored becomes a very bleak place indeed. There are parts of our world which we can look to in order to get a glimpse of what our society might be like if we ignored the purposes of God and pursued our own interests at the cost of our shared humanity. I want to highlight two areas where I think God's purposes are being ignored and where the consequences have led to a cheapening of human life: international conflict and acts of terror.

International conflict

The conflict in the Middle East between Israel and Lebanon in July 2006 highlighted once more for me the cheapening of human life which is now taken almost for granted by those in power. Unsurprisingly it is the stories of human interest, those stories of individual suffering, of the elderly and infirm unable to flee Katyusha rockets, of families sleeping on the floors of Beirut car parks and children bereaved of entire families through air strikes, that pull at our heart strings and grab our attention. But there are not resources enough in the media for telling the stories of each individual life that is lost. More than one thousand Lebanese and more than one hundred and twenty Israelis were killed in the conflict. The fact that some were from Hezbollah and others soldiers of the Israeli army does not mean their lives were worth any less than those of the civilians who also lost their lives. Yet for both sides the political and propagandist pictures presented of their opponents reinforced the gradual dehumanizing which takes place in conflict, where the lives of individuals are less valuable once they wear the label of terrorist, soldier or militant, and where the deaths of innocents are regretted in the same breath as the next volley of rockets are launched or air sorties scrambled.

While militarism succeeds in dehumanizing individuals, genocide succeeds in dehumanizing whole tribes. So it is for the people of Sudan, where at the time of writing the situation in Darfur is now reaching the levels of slaughter last seen in Serbia and Rwanda. Edmund Burke's words that 'for evil to triumph it requires only good men to do nothing' serve as condemnation for the wandering interest of western governments. As a newspaper editorial noted:

> Once again, there has been a reliance on peacekeepers, when in fact what was needed was peacemakers. The frustration is that peacemaking, i.e. the addressing of the problems that lead to violence, and acting robustly when conflict threatens, is far cheaper and more effective than trying to rebuild a country after war has run its course.[11]

In the absence of an effective UN intervention in Sudan, the suffering will continue. The UN has lacked the will to intervene and the African Union has lacked the means. Until there is an effective intervention by the United Nations in Darfur, which would be entirely legal and proper under international law by virtue of Security Council resolution 1706, our collective inaction on this issue will lead to the triumph of evil over and above God's purposes for that place.

Acts of terror

The second area where I believe God's purposes are not only being ignored but turned on their head is that of so-called 'Islamic terrorism'. A religious person who commits acts of terror denies the faith they appear to profess. By treating God's creation with contempt through the murdering of others, and in the case of suicide bombers self-contempt, those who commit acts of terror both usurp and pervert the fundamental tenets of faith in the most basic denial of the faith possible, by killing others in God's very name. Martyrs witness to their faith by their commitment to love and service, not by killing themselves and murdering others in the process.

Some of those who commit acts of terror have been described as 'Islamic fundamentalists' or even as 'Islamic fascists'. These are unhelpful terms to use, not least because they further alienate those who commit these hideous crimes through the use of terms which are Christian in origin, in the case of fundamentalists, and political in origin, in the case of fascism. It is dangerous to use these terms, which imply that the aggressive tendencies of certain strains of Islam are imported rather than indigenous. The simple adding of these disparate terms to Islam does not describe the motivation or purpose of these criminals, so they have little use and add little to our understanding. Rather, I believe the term to use for those committing acts of terror and those who seek to pervert the Islamic faith is 'Salafi Jihadists'. Salafis idealize an uncorrupted, pure Islamic community. In their rejection of all forms of Islamic scholarship in favour of a politically driven agenda, Salafi Jihadists reject the reality of God's creation for a fantasy. Their starting point is victimhood, especially against the West and Christianity. The violence of those who commit acts of terror is fed less by the clash of civilizations or belief than by its lack, and the insult to God that western disbelief represents. And sadly individual choice can justify anything, including murder and acts of terror. Knowledge for its own sake has become a power of destruction.

The history of the interpretation of *jihad* in Islam is a long one, with a very positive emphasis on spiritual growth, and on development as a process of self-denial, in the battle of wills and achievement of peace. However, for the modern-day Salafi Jihadists, who define themselves through acts of mass destruction and terror, *jihad* has taken on a whole new meaning, and the God who it claims to serve has become too small. For the God of the Salafi Jihadist has become far removed from the God of Islam. The love of God, the love of neighbour, whether in or out of the *ummah* (community of believers), and care of God's creation have all been repudiated by the acts of terror carried out by the Salafi Jihadist. In Islam Allah is 'all powerful and all merciful', yet for the Salafi Jihadist there is no mercy or power in the indiscriminate acts of terror. There is only destruction. The merciful character of a creator God has been left aside in favour of a new small god, leading to a perversion of Islam. Hence, rather than uncovering the purposes of God, the texts of the Qur'an are abused and selectively applied by the Salafi Jihadists, so that the suicide bomber acts in the name of the smallest of gods, while those who deal with the aftermath of the bombers' handiwork in Iraq, Israel and Afghanistan demonstrate God's love for his creation rather than the Salafi Jihadists' mutilation of it.

There is always a danger when making comments about 'Jihadists' that the charge of Islamaphobia follows close behind. So let me be clear. I am not by any means talking about all of Islam or all Muslims here. Indeed, as a faith community, Christians should recognize that one of the biggest contributions of the Muslim community in Britain has been its denial of the secularist call that faith should be privatized and should be regarded as a minority occupation. It has often been Muslims, as well as leaders of other faiths, who have joined with Christians in refusing to accept the creeping secularization that would replace 'Christmas' with 'Winterval', and remove references to faith from public noticeboards for fear of causing offence. It is both my view and my experience that most British Muslims do not feel threatened by our Christian moral foundations but by the cynicism of secularized culture that denies its own foundations. What they object to is the attempt to build human society without God. And so, given the choice between the two, they prefer a faith environment, even one which they do not share, to that of a secularist state. This is something which those who seek to remove offence continuously fail to comprehend or understand. Many, and I include myself in this, cannot understand how secularists who were shaped by the Christian gospel dislike the culture that nurtured them. Reason and human worth are at the very core of the Christian gospel, and that is precisely why, beyond the obvious historical facts, Christianity is the true foundation of British culture and values. And so my plea to all Muslims in this country is the words of Jesus Christ, who to you is a prophet and to me a saviour:

> You have heard that it was said, 'You shall love your neighbour and hate your enemy'. But I say to you, Love your enemies and pray for those who persecute you, so that you may be children of your Father in heaven; for he makes his sun rise on the evil and on the good, and sends rain on the righteous and on the unrighteous. For if you love those who love you, what reward do you have? . . . Be perfect, therefore, as your heavenly Father is perfect.   (Matthew 5.43–46a, 48)

During my prayer vigil and fast for peace in the Middle East, when I pitched a tent for a week in August 2006 in York Minster, I prayed with many people who came to show their support and solidarity for the victims of violence there. At the end of one of our hourly prayer sessions a 5-year-old lad, visibly upset, came up to me with his mother and said, 'Thank you for what you are doing. I am very upset with all the killings. Why didn't they get it sorted by talking?' A teenager asked, 'Why didn't God stop it? Where was he when people were killing each other?' 'He was being violated,' I replied to her. 'God was being violated.' I asked her: 'Do you remember Elijah and the wind, the earthquake and the fire?' 'Yes,' she said. 'God was not in them, but in a gentle, still voice.' God's voice is to be heard in the cry of an 8-year-old Lebanese girl, injured and orphaned, who had lost her eye in an air-strike, and in the voice of an 85-year-old Israeli woman, sick, poor and unable to move out of reach of the Katyusha rockets. Where is God? Surely he is being violated with those who are damaged by the consequences of violence, and being diminished with those who enact it.

Conclusion

So how might we overcome these obstacles to uncovering the purposes of God and establish our trust in a loving God, love of neighbour and caring for creation? With regard to the devaluing of life and humanity in international conflict, I will readily admit that there will always be issues of self-defence and timing with regard to intervention, and I am not about to circumvent the continuing debates surrounding the Christian theory of a just war. However, I am now convinced more than ever that violence is not the way in which we will win over our enemies. We must, each and every one of us, hold responsibility for seeking peace in our own time, in our own streets and in our own homes, as well as continuing to pray for the world. We must look at our own nation, our own children growing up in a society which does not always foster inclusion and generosity as a priority. It is surely fear and anxiety which leads to aggression. We must build a sense of safety. If we seek for others an integrity and legitimacy of civil society, we ourselves must strive to think about our own.

With regard to acts of terror, we must support any and all international efforts to restart the shattered peace process in the Middle East. The events of July 2006, in the Lebanon, Israel, the United States and Britain have demonstrated that we cannot afford any longer to leave the issues of the Middle East in the pending tray of unresolved business. There is no greater recruiting sergeant for would-be Salafi Jihadists than the conflict in the Middle East. Without urgent action on our part, for their sakes and our own, the spiral of violence that has lasted longer than the whole of my lifetime – and I was born in 1949 – will continue unabated, as new generations become mired in the enmity of their forefathers. The challenge for the international community is to make peace in the Middle East a priority for the sake of us all, and to sacrifice their own self-interest in the short term for the prize of sustainable peace.

As in all conflicts great and small, both sides have acquired supporters and protagonists. We as humans are prone to divide into camps named 'for' and 'against'. Christians must continue to struggle to find ways to create communities which transcend tribalism, where we strive to love one another as God loves us. We must not give in to the fear which is in all of us, but must seek to fan the spark of divine humanity which we all possess. So allow me to finish by reflecting on how I think each of us, and I include myself in this as much as anyone else, can learn how to trust in a loving God, love our neighbour and care for God's creation.

In the parable of the sheep and the goats in Matthew 25, Jesus was telling his disciples that if you want to meet God face to face, the nearest you are going to come to it on this planet is to look into the faces of your brothers and sisters – and especially your sisters and brothers who have been declared unrighteous, unclean, unacceptable. It is not that we find God there; it is that God finds us there. That is where our faith is nurtured and bears fruit. There, where we expect to meet monsters, we meet God instead. The opportunity to serve God lies there among the prisoners who have been reckoned to be least deserving of any service at all.

We are called to die to the values of the world – the greed for wealth, status and power, as well as to our psychological tendencies: our desires and compulsions for success, to be loved, to be held in esteem, to be acclaimed by those in our group, to have power and control over others. It is a call to disarm ourselves, to die to our plans and let God's plans and ways take hold of us.

I have come to believe that when I shall come face to face with 'the wounded Healer', who bears the marks of love, he will ask me, 'Sentamu, where are your tears for me to wipe away? Where are your wounds of love received through loving and laying down your life for me and my brothers and sisters – the hungry, thirsty, stranger, naked, sick prisoner?' If we throw ourselves on the grace of God and seek his purposes, our vocation – while never pitching our tent in the valley of relativism – is to see everyone, people of faith and none, not as enemies but as beloved neighbours and friends. All made in the image and likeness of God: a God who is Christlike.

Bishop Lesslie Newbigin is, for me, a great interpreter of the three things we must say about Christ and salvation today; how we relate Christianity to a society that has other faiths present. He said we must be:

- exclusive in the sense of affirming the unique truth of the revelation in Jesus Christ, but not in the sense of denying the possibility of salvation to those outside the Christian faith.
- inclusive in the sense of refusing to limit the saving grace of God to Christians, but not in the sense of viewing other religions as salvific.

- pluralist in the sense of acknowledging the gracious work of God in the lives of all human beings, but not in the sense of denying the unique and decisive nature of what God has done in Jesus Christ.[12]

It is from the cross that the light of God's love shines forth upon the world in its fullest splendour. Let us strive to hold on to both the glory of heaven and the brokenness of humanity. In our worship of God and serving our neighbour, may God help us to infect the world with his righteousness. We can nurture love, foster courage and seek wisdom; we can choose not to accept sentimentality, leave foolhardiness unchallenged or lapse into cowardice.

This brings me to an end. And what does it all come to? Surely this: that if we seek the meaning of truth and justice, we cannot find it by argument and debate, nor by reading and thinking, but only, in the words of the Book of Common Prayer, 'by the maintenance of true religion and virtue'. If religion perishes in the land, truth and justice will also. My hope and message to all of us is that, in a world of short cuts, deception and death, may we seek and find the Way which is of Truth and brings Life.

Notes

1 David Kenning, 'Review of the National Communications of the Church of England' (2000), at www.cofe.anglican.org/info/papers/communicationsreportandannexes.doc (accessed 13 September 2006).
2 See the Shelter report, *40 Years On*. It can be accessed through the Shelter website at www.shelter.org.uk.
3 I am grateful for the articles in Transformational Business Network – using business to bring spiritual and physical transformation to the world – at www.tbnetwork.org. Articles by Kris Coppock.

4 A. G. Gardiner, *The Life of George Cadbury* (London: Cassell, 1949).

5 A. Vernon, *A Quaker Business Man* (London: George Allen & Unwin Ltd, 1958).

6 *Faith in the City: A Call to Action by Church and Nation* was published in 1985 by the Archbishop of Canterbury's Commission on Urban Priority Areas.

7 Church of England Urban Commission on Life and Faith, *Faithful Cities: A Call for Celebration, Vision and Justice* (London: Church House Publishing/Methodist Publishing House, 2006).

8 In Alan Stephens and Raphael Walden (eds), *For the Sake of Humanity: Essays in Honour of Clemens N. Nathan* (Leiden: Martinus Nijhoff, 2006).

9 Tom Kickey, University of Michigan.

10 As quoted in Lord Denning, *The Influence of Religion on Law* (London: Lawyers' Christian Fellowship, 1989).

11 *Church Times*, 8 September 2006.

12 Lesslie Newbigin, *The Gospel in a Pluralist Society* (London: SPCK, 1989), pp. 182–3.

2

God and our public life: a scriptural wisdom

DAVID F. FORD

The essays in this book are mainly concerned with the contribution to our public life of scriptural texts, Jewish, Christian and Muslim. As a Christian academic and as someone involved in interfaith relations, particularly between Judaism, Christianity and Islam, I want to put forward several points: first, that our public life needs whatever wisdom we can find, whether religious or secular; second, that the Bible is a rich source of such wisdom; third, that our religious and secular world needs frameworks, patterns, settlements and institutions within which this and other wisdoms (both religious and secular) can be put forward, learned, taught, explained, discussed, disputed, deliberated about and have practical effects in public life; fourth, that in the world of the early twenty-first century the ways of doing this that have been worked out in Britain have considerable potential both at home and abroad, but that they need to be both critiqued and developed much further; fifth, that there is a special need to do fuller justice in the public sphere to religious intensities, those deep and powerful convictions, understandings, desires, community attachments, habits and practices that are at the heart of each tradition, and that one vital way of doing so is by thorough engagement with the scriptural texts that are at the core of their identities; and finally, that because religious intensities in the public sphere rightly give rise to deep fears of fanaticism, divisive confrontation and bloody conflict, one of the greatest needs is for the healthy intensity of passionately wise faith. My main illustration will be the practice of scriptural reasoning with which I have been involved for more than a decade.[1]

Wisdom in public life

I begin with some very brief remarks on the huge topic of wisdom in public life. I take it for granted that we need as much wisdom as possible and as little foolishness as possible. By wisdom in public life, in very broad terms, I mean a combination of rich understanding, discernment and good judgement relating to people, ideas, situations, institutions and traditions; far-sighted decision-making among practical possibilities; and all this within a commitment to the long-term, transgenerational flourishing of a society in relation to other societies and to the natural environment. I hope that it is uncontroversial to desire more of that sort of wisdom.

What is more controversial is where such wisdom is to be found, but I will just state my own commonsense conclusion. It is this: that any set of convictions, ideas and practices, whether religious or secular, that has played a significant role in shaping a tradition or community over many years, is likely to have some worthwhile wisdom to contribute to public life. At the very least, we should try to make sure that this belief is tested to the full and that the conditions are created within which the contributions of various wisdoms are encouraged. I think this is a matter of common sense, especially in a democracy. As a Christian I would also ground it in a biblical understanding of wisdom. The Bible is notably hospitable to traditions of wisdom in the Ancient Near East and in the Hellenistic and Roman civilizations, and does not see God as confining wisdom to believers; there are many instances of wisdom arising outside Israel and the Church. The practice of the early Church and most later traditions was to engage appreciatively as well as critically with thought and practice in their surrounding cultures. And from within their own traditions many Jews, Muslims, Hindus and others would make similar points about how their wisdom has been drawn from many sources. To say that no tradition has a monopoly on wisdom is not to be a relativist: in theological terms it is simply to believe in the providence and generosity of God.

Biblical wisdom for public life

I will be equally brief on the equally huge topic of the Bible as a source of such wisdom for public life. There are as many ways of approaching this as there are Christian traditions, with conclusions and practices differing deeply. I simply want to note what it is in the Bible that makes it virtually inevitable that Christians will bring it to bear in public life; indeed, I would say that they are being unfaithful and irresponsible if they fail to do so. This is the basic biblical reality that God is the Creator of all and constantly concerned with every aspect of life: human and non-human; public and private; individual and social; religious, cultural, economic and political; past, present and future. In all of these spheres, God and the purposes of God really matter, and since the Bible is the core Christian text for identifying who God is and what God's purposes are, the Bible really matters.

Yet to say that Christians must for these reasons bring the Bible to bear on public life is not the same as to say that this necessarily produces wisdom that will contribute to the flourishing of society today. Christian history has many examples (from slavery and sexism to the crusades and apartheid) of scripture being applied to public life in ways that have led to injustice, violence and misery. The further vital ingredient is that the interpretation of scripture has to be wise. I will say more about this later, but one element in wise interpretation is that it tries to take the reality of the contemporary situation into account, and to this I now turn.

Settlements in a religious and secular world

In September 2006 I was in New York at the Clinton Global Initiative. This is a remarkable attempt to bring together non-governmental organizations (NGOs) with those willing to donate large sums of money in order to tackle major world problems. The focus in the two meetings so far has been on five areas: poverty; climate change; health; governance and transparency; and religious and ethnic conflict. At the first meeting in 2005 about US$2.5 billion was raised for projects; the total for the second is around US$5 billion. This is a new idea – an NGO that is global in scope, headed by Bill Clinton and brokering funding for other NGOs around the world on a scale way beyond what most governments do. For our purposes I want to draw on it to make two points.

The first is a reflection on the fact that one of the concerns is with religion. I suspect that twenty years ago this might not have been the case. Before the fall of Soviet communism both the capitalist and communist worlds tended to write religion out of their scenarios of the future. Today, projections of a simply secular future seem less persuasive. The shift in perception is probably mainly due to what is called militant Islam, beginning with the Iranian Revolution and climaxing in the destruction of the World Trade Center in 2001. But one might argue that this perception is just catching up with the reality obscured by the expansion of communism earlier in the twentieth century and by the influence, especially in the media and education, of a largely secularized western-educated elite throughout that period. Probably between 4 and 5 billion of the world's more than 6 billion people are directly involved with a religion today, and this picture seems unlikely to change a great deal during the rest of the twenty-first century. So during the lifetimes of all of us now alive we would do well to reckon seriously with religions as shapers of our world, for worse or for better. This does not mean that we have a purely religious world with which to deal; rather it is simultaneously both religious and secular in complex ways. There are important issues between the religions; but there are also overlapping issues between each of the religions and the various secular understandings and forces.

This is not a new situation, and we would be wise to take account of the ways such relationships have been handled in the past. This brings me to the second point from the Clinton Global Initiative. One of the sessions in the section on Religious and Ethnic Conflict had a panel with an Englishman, a Frenchman and an American. As they spoke about religion and politics the Frenchman resisted any suggestion that religions should be taken seriously as religions within the political sphere: problems were traced mainly to economic causes, and he was confident that if poverty were dealt with effectively the unrest in French cities would disappear. The American (who was also a Muslim) insisted that the religions needed to contribute to public discourse but that the American separation of church and state was healthy. The Englishman, John Battle MP (the former Prime

Minister Tony Blair's special adviser on interfaith matters), told stories of his own involvement with religious communities in his Leeds constituency, and evoked a complex settlement in which religious bodies were seen as stakeholders in society with whom the government and other public bodies were in constant communication and negotiation, and whose identities could be affirmed by such means as state-supported faith schools.

It was as if each was representing his own nation's settlement, developed over centuries. To pass judgements on such complex achievements, each worked out in special circumstances, is dangerous, but I will risk it in summary form.

I think that in the current world situation the French secularist solution is the least satisfactory. It, like the others, is understandable in historical terms – working out the epochal, often bloody confrontation between the French Revolution and Roman Catholicism – but its practical exclusion of religions from the public sphere (including state schools and universities) is in effect the establishment of a state ideology that is not neutral in relation to religion but is suspicious, critical and often hostile. It is not well suited to a religious and secular world.

The American separation of church and state is far more benign with regard to the religions, and in fact religion plays a major role in American politics. But there has been a tendency to try to use the separation to create a neutral public space, where it is illegitimate to draw explicitly on religious sources. This 'lowest common denominator' public square (expressed, for example, in banning official recognition of any particular religious symbols, holidays or practices and refusing to let state schools teach religious education or state universities teach theology as well as religious studies) is increasingly being criticized, even by secular thinkers such as

Jeffrey Stout of Princeton University, who see it as an impoverishment of public life. Both religious and secular traditions should be able to contribute in their distinctive ways to public debate rather than reducing all discourse to a secularized lowest common denominator.[2]

The best of the American situation is what happens in Britain. Britain's particular history has kept religion involved in public life, sometimes controversially. I think it is to the credit of the present Labour government that it has usually resisted pressures from those members of its own party who have more sympathy with secularist, often atheist, ideologies and would favour a French-style settlement. Yet there are many forces in Britain that push for, and even achieve in limited spheres, settlements that do not take religions seriously and have more in common with French or American patterns. It is all too easy to imagine scenarios in which they would become more dominant. Britain also comes out rather poorly in comparative studies of the relative alienation of the Muslim minority from the rest of society.

There is at present, however, a window of opportunity for strengthening the British settlement in ways that could be important far beyond this country. In global terms, Britain has the conditions for pioneering work in shaping a religious and secular society that draws on the resources within each of the traditions for peaceful living and working together. We have an extraordinary range of religious communities in a society that has also experienced intense secularization. There is no widespread confidence that 'the secular project' can adequately resource this society in areas such as personal and family life, ethics and politics, health and environment, civic and international responsibilities. So where is wisdom to be found for the shaping of this society in the twenty-first century? I see a prime source in the renewal of particular religious communities, always beginning with one's own; and for Judaism, Christianity and Islam that must involve a scriptural wisdom.

Why is the British settlement at its best well suited to this? I think it is because it works within what one might call a minimal secular and religious framework that enables mutual public space. This has been shaped over many centuries and is constantly open to renegotiation; the main concern at present is about the place of Islam, though I think that there should also be far more attention to Christianity. The framework is minimal in that it refuses to impose either a particular religious solution or a particular secular solution and so lives by ongoing negotiation rather than by appeal to a fixed constitution or principles. It therefore helps to create a mutual public space with possibilities for shared discussion, dialogue, education, deliberation and collaboration; in contrast to the French tendency towards strictly secular public space and the American tendency towards neutral public space.

The British challenge

If this description is roughly true, the big question is how well the various traditions or communities are able to meet the challenge to be contributors to the flourishing of society through drawing on their richest resources in mutual engagement with each other. Not all will wish to take part in that way, but I would judge that each of the main forms of the Abrahamic faiths has good internal reasons for doing so. I sketched a Christian biblical rationale above and suggested that the others have their own analogous versions, also rooted in God as Creator of all and desiring the good of all. But that is quite abstract, and the fact that these rationales have been there for centuries, during which the Abrahamic faiths have often been in conflict with each other, makes it clear that such a potential convergence need have few practical results. So what might help make the vital connections between those crucial elements: the core scripturally shaped and distinct identities of Judaism, Christianity and Islam; the mutual engagement between those distinct identities (and others); and the common good of our society?

In general terms there are obviously a great many ways of making those connections. A look around Britain at present reveals a huge number of examples of good practice that in various ways bring together those elements of particular faith, mutual engagement and concern for the flourishing of society as a whole. It has been my privilege as Director of the Cambridge Inter-Faith Programme[3] to learn more about these ways, including many that seldom or never receive publicity. There are local, regional, national and international initiatives; they take place between religious communities and local government as well as national government, in education, healthcare, business, politics, sport, the arts, the media and other spheres; there are exciting developments in chaplaincy around the country; there are networks that link together participants in diverse spheres; and the approaches in all these are immensely varied. Perhaps most important of all are the many testimonies to friendships across faith and other boundaries; I am convinced that, whatever happens in groups, networks, institutions and movements, the supreme sign of fruitfulness is the formation of friendships. Among all the possible interfaith examples, I want to choose just one for fuller discussion. I will introduce it autobiographically.

David F. Ford

From Birmingham interfaith discussion to joint study of scriptures

I spent fifteen years in my first job teaching in the Theology Department in the University of Birmingham. It was a formative time in many ways: being apprenticed to the trade of teaching undergraduates and postgraduates in a university; conversing intensively over many years with colleagues; living in the inner city of Birmingham, and there being fully part of a local parish for the first time in my life; learning about urban regeneration through being part of a housing association; facing the challenges of education by being governor of an inner-city comprehensive school; and experiencing in many other ways the life and energy of Britain's second city. It was also the place where for the first time (apart from a year as a student in America when I had two close friends among the New York Jewish community) I really met members of other faiths.

Birmingham offered a multifaceted interfaith engagement: a house mosque two doors away from where I lived; a multifaith local community; some involvement with the Selly Oak Colleges' centres for the study of Judaism and the study of Islam, including their relations with Christianity; and above all three very different Christians for whom dialogue with other faiths was deeply part of their lives.

The first was Professor John Hick, whose home discussion group met once a month and frequently tackled his and other approaches to the religions. The more I discussed with him the less I was convinced by his form of pluralism, and least of all by his account of Christian faith.

The second was Bishop Lesslie Newbigin, who had spent many years as a missionary and later bishop in India and also served the International Missionary Council and the World

Council of Churches. He had developed a rich theology of mission and of how Christians might relate to other faiths with respect and love while also testifying to their own faith. On his return to teach in Birmingham he complemented this by a thorough engagement with secular western culture. He was a deeply impressive person, and his simultaneous concern for the religious and the secular rang true.

The third was perhaps the most influential, though the least widely known – Roger Hooker, who taught in Selly Oak Colleges and was later interfaith adviser to the Anglican Bishop of Birmingham. He had spent many years in India, learning Sanskrit and Hindi, and essential to his dialogue with Hindus was joint study of Hindu and Christian scriptures. I sensed at the time the fruitfulness of his way, but it was only some years later that I came to something similar by another route.

For me the problem about my Birmingham interfaith engagement was that it was largely issue-centred discussion with much conversation and some practical collaboration across faith boundaries, but it did not provide ways of sustaining the sort of intensive conversation over time that in other spheres creates the collegiality, collaboration and friendships that make a long-term difference. That new dimension happened unexpectedly after I had moved to Cambridge in 1991.

I used to travel most years to attend the American Academy of Religion (AAR) and there started sitting on the fringe of the meetings of a new group called 'Textual Reasoning'. These were Jewish text scholars and philosophers who had discovered that the text scholars knew their scriptures and Talmud, but often had little engagement with modern thought, while the philosophers were modern thinkers who had not studied the classic texts of their tradition. So they came together to study texts from both sides and also the writings of some modern Jewish thinkers, like Rosenzweig, Buber and Levinas, who had already tried to make the connections. A few other Christians and I found the meetings deeply exciting – full of scholarship, humour and passionate argument, constantly moving back and forth between premodernity, modernity and postmodernity, and often with a strong liturgical, ethical or political thrust. Eventually we Christians joined together with some of them to form a new group, called 'Scriptural Reasoning' – Jews and Christians studying the Tanakh and the Bible together.[4] Then a couple of years later we invited Muslims to join us. For the past decade we have had an international meeting twice a year at the AAR and in Cambridge, and local groups have started in many places in Britain and the USA, and in other countries.

Scriptural Reasoning: a new collegiality

The idea is very simple. We gather in small groups, ideally six- or nine-strong, with two or three from each tradition, and study and discuss texts from each scripture, usually on a common theme: justice and law, or worship, or money, or authority and leadership, or love, or land, or war and peace, or the future, or wisdom; or a particular figure such as Abraham, Jonah, Joseph, Jesus, or Mary; or a story; or a prayer; or a symbol – one that has recurred is the tent, which in these Middle Eastern texts has such resonances of desert hospitality and of divine presence. If there are several groups we have plenary discussions too, often about the issues that have arisen in the text study, or on the future applications and implications of this new Abrahamic practice. It is simple in conception, but the dynamics of such shared study and discussion can become quite complex. After ten years of attempting it, I feel that we are all still very much at the beginning, learning basics, testing approaches, finding out what is fruitful and what is not.

This is hardly surprising. Around the table are representatives of three traditions each of which within itself has many further traditions of interpretation of these rich texts, developed over hundreds of years, with energetic debates continuing today all around the world, often on very contentious issues. There are three scriptural languages, Hebrew, Greek and Arabic, with the addition of English as the usual common language. And while each tradition has its own forms of study, education and debate, there is almost nowhere in the world today where the three join together in collegiality year after year in order to study and discuss like this.

This collegiality is a key feature that goes well beyond my Birmingham experience of interfaith engagement. It enables trust, and often friendship, to be built. It also allows for deep differences to be faced. This sort of study does not usually lead to consensus but at its best allows for ongoing argument and the development in the group of what one might call a wisdom of dispute and disagreement. The result is not a set of agreed statements on the Trinity or on anything else, but enriched understanding across differences and commitment to a process of endless conversation, resourced by these endlessly generative scriptural texts. In this process one can be true to one's core identity, reading and sharing the scriptures witnessing to that identity, while also continually nourished by and answerable to those from one's own or other traditions.

This works best when it is not seen as mainly instrumental, a means to an end, however worthy, such as greater knowledge of texts, or better relations among the religions, or peace in the Middle East. It is of course good when there are good outcomes, and I will mention some in a minute.

But the God-centred character of all these scriptures means that the wisest way to enter into this study is to do it for God's sake. Each of the three traditions has its own, distinct yet related, ways of giving priority to God, honouring God, blessing or hallowing the name of God, respecting the mystery of God's active, holy presence among us. These texts are most liberating when they are read for the sake of God and God's purposes, even though we differ on just how God is to be identified.

This is immensely important for public life. Each of the Abrahamic faiths identifies idolatry as the most radical distortion and corruption of human life. To give ultimate status, honour and priority to whatever is not God – whether a race, a nation, a leader, an ideal, a gender, an ideology, a science, an economic system or even the whole of creation – harnesses immense religious energies often to devastating effect. The most insidious forms of idolatry are explicitly religious, distorted ways of identifying God or trying to harness God to one's own cause. The only reliable way of countering such idolatries is continually to seek the God beyond our constructions, to be open to correction, challenge and critique, and to sustain those practices of prayer, common life, study and debate that allow the truth to be recognized. What could be healthier for each of the Abrahamic faiths than to contribute to this by the shared study of scriptures? What could be healthier for our public life than for citizens within these faiths to be able to share their wisdom and together to work out ways of faithful, non-idolatrous service of the common good?

That is what is beginning to happen in little ways where scriptural reasoning is being developed by new groups in various contexts. At St Ethelburga's Centre for Peace and Reconciliation in London (outcome of a vision of Richard

Chartres, Bishop of London, after St Ethelburga's Church was partly destroyed by an IRA bomb) there is an actual tent, a modified Bedouin one, covered with Gore-Tex to keep out the rain (it was opened by Prince Charles in May 2006) on a piece of waste ground behind the centre, in which groups engage in scriptural reasoning. They are not mostly academics, but Muslim, Jewish and Christian citizens of London from many walks of life. They have worked out forms of study appropriate to them and materials to support the practice, including a website. In the autumn of 2006 they pioneered a course called 'FACT' (Faith and Citizenship Training) which integrates scriptural reasoning into a course for London rabbis, clergy and imams aimed at mutual understanding and collaboration in local communities.[5] Similar things have happened in schools through the Three Faiths Forum, whose Education Officer, Miriam Kaye, has initiated a programme called 'Tools 4 Trialogue' in which teenagers discuss the opinions of the three scriptures on authority and rebellion, dress and modesty and child–parent relationships.

The vision of such initiatives, whether in universities, schools or civic life, is not of instant fixes for conflicts whose roots go back centuries. It is rather more like trying to change the religious and secular 'ecology' by paying attention to fundamental matters that are the religious and cultural equivalents of clean water, well-cultivated soil, sound agricultural methods and an unpolluted environment. Wise interpretation of scriptures, helping to shape lives and communities before God and in line with the purposes of God, is a matter of transgenerational practices and the development of people, groups and institutions within the religious communities and between them. It is also something that profoundly challenges each of the traditions in their responses to modernity. I now turn to this, perhaps the most difficult matter of all.

The challenge of modernity

Each of the Abrahamic faiths has deep pre-modern roots. So, given the enormous transformations in every sphere of life in recent centuries (the complex phenomenon often labelled modernity), they have faced massive problems about how to respond. How to interpret their pre-modern scriptures is of course a vital part of this.

Those young Jewish philosophers and scholars of scripture and Talmud who began 'Textual Reasoning' and later helped form 'Scriptural Reasoning' are an instructive example of some of the main options. One of their principal concerns was with the renewal of Judaism after the Shoah/Holocaust. They saw their fellow Jews moving in three basic directions, none of which seemed adequate to them. Some responded to the trauma of genocide by intense distrust of the whole Gentile world that had tried to wipe them out. They opted for a renewed traditional orthodoxy, pre-modern or anti-modern in many ways, and separated themselves as much as possible from the rest of the world, religious and secular. Others responded to the trauma by deciding that there was no good future in distinctive Jewish identity and gave up on that, assimilating to modernity. Yet others opted for a Jewish identity that was largely ethnic, political and cultural rather than religious. The textual reasoners went for a different sort of option from any of these (and different too from the various mixtures and compromises between the extremes). They wanted to integrate three elements: first, deeper engagement with their roots, especially as represented in scripture, Talmud and Jewish liturgy; second, deeper involvement with non-Jewish people of faith, especially those from the Abrahamic traditions; and third, thorough critical and constructive engagement with modernity, aimed above all at compassionate healing of its pathologies, including those that opened the way for the Shoah.[6]

I see this integrated response as a pattern for both Christianity and Islam to follow and improvise upon in their own ways, which are bound to be distinctively different due to diverse scriptures, traditions of interpretation, traumatic historical experiences and much else. Each also has a great deal to learn from the other two about the three elements: interpreting scriptures, traditions and liturgies; dialogue across religious divisions; and coping with modernity. Wise response to modernity requires that whole ecology. The temptation is to go for more simple solutions. The vision is of nothing less than wiser Jewish faith, wiser Christian faith and wiser Muslim faith for the twenty-first century. This involves each of them taking their own core identities seriously through wise interpretation of their authoritative sources; taking each other seriously not as outsiders but as Abrahamic siblings who offer each other mutual hospitality, teaching and critique that can lead to friendship; and taking the developments and discourses of modernity seriously by attempting to discern together what in them is to be affirmed, what is to be rejected and what is to be healed and transformed.

What are the threats to developing wiser twenty-first-century faiths? For the past two centuries or more it has seemed, especially in the West, that the main threat came from atheist or agnostic secular understanding. It has been a time of comprehensive critiques of religion associated with names such as Feuerbach, Marx, Nietzsche, Freud, Darwin, Russell and their successors. These have succeeded in making atheism or agnosticism (at least practical atheism or practical agnosticism) the default position of many western-educated intellectuals (though most of them will not have engaged seriously with the cases made by both sides, and, usually, it is the cases made by intelligent, well-educated believers that are neglected). There has recently been a resurgence of explicit, combative atheism, such as that of Richard Dawkins, who has written a book on God as a delusion.[7]

Yet looking back over the past two and a half centuries, and paying attention to the way each new critique has been seen as deadly, it is remarkable how well religion has fared. Every apparently devastating argument has been replied to by counter-arguments. On both sides are people of comparable intelligence, education, sophistication, philosophical acuteness, historical scholarship or scientific ability. There are plenty of scientists who reject Dawkins' view of the atheist implications of science,[8] and plenty of philosophers who dispute his claim to a rationally convincing rejection of God.[9] My worry concerning Dawkins is not so much about his effects on religion (which has survived far more plausible critiques) as about the implications for science. His neat, self-certain ideological package (which, as many have remarked, has similarities to some of the fundamentalist religious ideologies that he attacks) is dangerous for the public perception of science. If science is associated in the public mind too closely with this contested and inadequate position, then when (as inevitably will happen) it is discredited or rendered less plausible, the risk is that science itself will be discredited, and a proper, modest confidence in its claims (which are so essential to a healthy modernity) will be undermined. Scientists would be wise to distance themselves now from the Dawkins package.

The secular critiques of religion have to be taken seriously and given proper attention, but I see far greater threats to wise faith in our century coming from within each of the religious traditions themselves. The pathologies of the religions are of course made worse by their mirror opposites in the secular sphere, as the extremes reinforce each other. Unwise, fundamentalist religious dogmatisms feed off unwise, fundamentalist secularist ideologies, and vice versa. Such polemical, vehement intensities make it very tempting to say: 'A plague on both your houses. Let us have moderation in all things and banish intensities from the public sphere.'

I would argue that this is partly right at one level but that, at a deeper level, it is unwise. The level at which it is partly right is that of a minimal framework for peaceful public life. Religious intensities of a fundamentalist kind (like secular intensities, whether fascist, communist or scientistic) tend to want to dominate the public sphere on their own terms. In our sort of society and world this is a recipe for endless, divisive conflict and even bloodshed. The wars of religion in Europe showed this, and the hard-earned wisdom that helped to create our settlements in Britain, France or the USA must not be forgotten. We need what I have called a minimal religious and secular framework, constantly open to renegotiation in the light of new situations (such as that created by large-scale Muslim immigration), but insistent on the priority of the common good.

Yet I would also argue that the sort of framework we have in Britain at its best allows the intensities to contribute peacefully in the public sphere. The corruption of the best is the worst. The answer to distorted intensities is not to banish the intensity of commitment to a God of peace who wants the good of all. As a Christian I would say that this 'best' involves whole-hearted love of God and passionate dedication to the purposes of God in private and in public life. The crucial thing is for that love and dedication to be as wise as possible. I know many Jews and Muslims who would make parallel affirmations. They do not want a 'moderation' that stops them being utterly committed Jews and Muslims; they do want a passionate wisdom that directs such intensity towards peace and the common good (although this is only likely to succeed if it includes a wisdom of moderation in most things). To take an analogy from another realm of passion: a couple does not ensure marital peace by banning sexual passion and the other intensities (including those of argument) that can nourish lifelong devotion to each other. In religion, as in marriage, there is a wisdom of desire, commitment, love and argument.

I think of two examples from October 2006. Some of you may have followed the controversy sparked off by Pope Benedict XVI's Regensburg lecture, with its controversial quotation of comments on Islam by a Byzantine emperor. For me the most fascinating and hopeful part of that incident was the detailed commentary on the lecture written by the Muslim philosopher and theologian Dr Aref Ali Nayed, which was then responded to by the Catholic theologian Alessandro Martinetti, to whom in turn Dr Nayed replied.[10] I see Dr Nayed reaching after and beginning to develop a wisdom of respectful dispute in the midst of the intensities of controversy, but one that has its own, deeply Muslim, intensity of devotion to the wisdom, peace and compassion of Allah.

The second example was the visit to Cambridge in October 2006 of the Grand Mufti of Egypt, Dr Ali Gomaa, from Al Azhar University. His public lecture was an exposition of Islam that rejects the violent extremists but is also passionately committed to Allah and the revelation in the Qur'an. His long conversations with the Cambridge Inter-Faith Programme in private included detailed discussion of Muslim traditions that can resource wise interpretation of the Qur'an for which the mercy and compassion of Allah are utterly central and pervasive.

I could multiply examples, but I want to conclude with some remarks about my own faith tradition.

Towards wiser Christian faith

As a Christian I am apprehensive about the danger that is posed in the twenty-first century by my own tradition, Christianity. In worldly terms we are the most powerful of the faiths. We have more numbers (sometimes estimated at around 2 billion), more wealth, more lethal weapons, more control of media, more top-rank educational institutions, and so on, than any other tradition. Of course all that power is involved complexly with secular and other interests, but for now my main point is simply that Christians are immensely powerful in the public sphere and if they go badly wrong then there can be devastating effects on our world. Christians above all therefore need to be committed, for the sake of God, to working out a wisdom of faith that serves the purposes of God and the peaceful flourishing of our world.

Such a wisdom is bound to have many dimensions and elements. This book points to one of the most important. Christianity's core identity is inseparable from the testimony of the Bible, and its wisdom must be in line with the Bible if it is to be genuinely Christian. But what is in line with the Bible? Answering that would take many lectures, even whole libraries of books, but in what remains I want to comment on a few verses from one of the greatest works of wisdom ever written, the book of Job, verses that give some clues to the sort of wise faith most needed today.

At the beginning of the book Job is portrayed as immensely wealthy, wise and faithful to God, but then he is tested in the most extreme way; his whole world collapses and he is traumatized. The key to his testing is in Satan's question to God: 'Does Job fear God for nothing?' (Job 1.9, NRSV), or is he afraid for the wealth, health, children, social standing and the meaningfulness of life? Is his a faith in God for God's sake?

In chapter 3 he cries out in utter affliction and despair, then engages in the great debate with his friends. This can be read as both the testing and the maturing of his faith – a wise faith in the making. In chapter 23 verses 1–9 we are given some clues to the vital elements in this maturing faith. 'Then Job answered: "Today also my complaint is bitter; his hand is heavy despite my groaning"' (23.1–2). This is an utterly realistic faith, facing the facts of his situation and full of complaint and lament, the sort of faith that resonates with Jesus' cry from the cross: 'My God, my God, why have you forsaken me?' (Mark 15.34). Mature faith in this God is no escape from reality, whether personal or public.

'Oh, that I knew where I might find him, that I might come even to his dwelling!' (Job 23.3). Cries of longing, of desire for God, run through what Job says. These are perhaps the deepest clue to his faith – his unquenchable desire for God. Here is the answer to Satan's question: Job cries out not to get back his wealth or his children or his social standing or even his untroubled, unproblematic theology; he cries out to get God back! And that seems to be what pleases God most, because at the end he is commended by God for speaking right of God, unlike his friends.

'I would lay my case before him, and fill my mouth with arguments. I would learn what he would answer me, and understand what he would say to me' (23.4–5). Job is constantly hypothesizing (and these are some of the milder hypotheses about how he might relate to God), exploring possibilities, stretching his imagination in his relationship with God. The poetry is daring, and so too is the theology it expresses. We do not attain a wise faith without all our faculties being mobilized in a wholehearted relationship with God, and that includes our imagination, our capacity for what might be called faith in the subjunctive mood of 'maybe', 'might be' and 'perhaps'.

Job questions, 'Would he contend with me in the greatness of his power?' (23.6). His faith allows him to ask the most radical questions of his friends, of himself, of the way the world is and of God. It is a vital mark of wise faith that it can question and be questioned, honestly search and be searched. Job's faith is no neat package or formula: it confronts life, suffering and the confusions of life, and it is open to being challenged.

Then in verse 8 we find realism about the mystery of God. This God is not in our control, and does not necessarily let us know God as we would like. 'If I go forward, he is not there; or backward, I cannot perceive him; on the left he hides, and I cannot behold him; I turn to the right, but I cannot see him' (23.8–9). Not seeing, not knowing, is a large ingredient of wise faith.

Job continues with a basic affirmation: 'But he knows the way that I take; when he has tested me, I shall come out like gold' (23.10). The secret of faith lies not so much in our knowing as in our being known by God; not so much in our questioning and testing as in our being questioned and tested; not so much in our desiring as in our being desired and loved.

Then in verses 11 and 12 there is a further crucial element of faith, the imperative, the commandment of God: 'My foot has held fast to his steps; I have kept his way and have not turned aside. I have not departed from the commandment of his lips; I have treasured in my bosom the words of his mouth.'

What is the shape of wise faith that emerges from this and other passages in Job? It weaves together open-eyed, realistic description, a passionate desire for God and doing God's will, a daring imagination, radical questioning, recognition of the mystery of God and of the limits of our knowledge, and the embracing reality and priority of God's knowing, desiring, surprising, questioning and willing.

But how do all those go together? Which takes priority at any particular time? This is the wisdom that Job has to learn a step at a time, as he copes with the intensity of his suffering and struggles to make sense of his life and of God. Alongside him we are given his friends as object lessons in what is judged at the end of the book to be foolish faith. They do have faith in God and are orthodox in what they say of God, but they never seem really to hear Job, and their faith does not lead them to grapple compassionately with what so disturbs him. They offer him neat packages of faith, much of it classic teaching about God and God's ways, but simple repetitions of the formulae of wisdom that have worked in the past do not meet this new situation and the dilemma of this particular person. Theirs is not a faith that can wrestle with trauma or respond to the new; it tries to stay the same, repeat the tradition and, on that basis, to make affirmations and issue imperatives. However, there is little sense of searching or being searched, little daring imagination and, above all, little intensity of desire for God.

The longing of Job to be vindicated and to hear and see God is finally honoured by God, but when God speaks out of the whirlwind (Job 38) God does not give answers; there are no neat packages. Much of God's speech is mind-blowing new questions to Job that set Job's questions and laments in the context of the amazing creation of God. The lesson seems to be: creation is not there just for the use of Job or humans – 'Is the wild ox willing to serve you?' (39.9) – it is created for its own sake; therefore how much more is God its creator to be revered for God's own sake! The ultimate dignity and glory of human beings is to glory in God, glory in creation and therefore, of course, to glory in each other. The final chapter of the book has Job in awe before God, Job forgiving and praying for his friends, and around him a renewed, transgenerational community of well-being, generosity, compassion and beauty. It is an ideal picture of wise living before God after trauma.

One of the reasons why the book of Job has been the subject of so much discussion during the past century has been because of the totalitarianisms, wars, genocides, terrorism and other traumas that the world has gone through, added to the massively disorienting changes of modernity. In this situation no simple repetition of past faith will do, and those who attempt it repeat the folly of Job's friends. In public life the calling of Christians might be seen as to seek in faith a wisdom that imitates Job. We will cry out before God the truth of our times, however painful, and try to describe the world truthfully (using arts, humanities, sciences and other aids) in the light of God; we will question deeply and persistently, above all asking about the purposes of God today; we will stretch our political, social and economic imaginations to envision the ways we might, with others, serve the coming of God's kingdom; and above all we will seek to shape our lives and those of our churches around the desire for God and God's future. That undertaking could only be formed and sustained with the help of wise reading of scripture. Such reading is rooted in the desire for God in prayer and worship, draws on all relevant scholarly disciplines, learns from pre-modern, modern and contemporary readers, studies with people of other faiths, and never ceases to learn from the wisdom of Job.

Prospect

Finally, a comment on the future of religion in Europe: I have just finished reading for a publisher the typescript of a book on religion in Europe today by a distinguished contemporary historian. It is a masterly survey, full of facts, statistics and interpretations that largely convinced me, and the picture he draws of the current situation is in many ways surprising. I want to conclude with two of the future possibilities he thinks likely.

One is that, for Islam, Europe will be a place of creative transformation and intellectual renewal, with beneficial results far beyond Europe. The other is more surprising: that European Christianity is showing remarkable signs of vitality. It could well be incubating something of great importance for Europe and for the rest of the world. It has more than survived amid European secularism; many of its strands have, under intense pressure, been learning well how to cope with modernity, and also how to engage with other faiths while remaining true to core beliefs and practices; because of immigrant Christians European Christianity is a microcosm of global Christianity; the public mood is more open to religion than it has been for many decades; and the lessons of history are that a widespread conviction that Christianity is in decline or under threat or doomed is the best indicator that a major expansion or revival is about to happen. Think of Europe on the eve of the Reformation; or Methodism in eighteenth-century England; or, in the nineteenth century, the worldwide missionary movement, the second evangelical revival and the Catholic devotional revolution; or, in the twentieth century, the greatest religious movement in history, Pentecostalism and its charismatic cousins, involving perhaps over 300 million people. But, think also of the distortions and dangers in all of those.

If that author is right, then the concerns expressed here – about the quality of faith, especially Christian faith, and about the wisdom of its contributions to public life – become even more urgent.

Notes

1 For further thoughts on many of the above points, see David F. Ford, *Christian Wisdom: Desiring God and Learning in Love* (Cambridge: Cambridge University Press, 2007).
2 Jeffrey Stout, *Democracy and Tradition* (Princeton: Princeton University Press, 2004).
3 Website: www.divinity.cam.ac.uk/cip.
4 See David F. Ford and C. C. Pecknold (eds), *The Promise of Scriptural Reasoning* (Oxford: Blackwell, 2006).
5 The Cambridge Inter-Faith Programme and London Metropolitan University have joined with St Ethelburga's in academically resourcing this.
6 For further discussion of this, with references to relevant literature, see Ford, *Christian Wisdom*, chapters 3 and 4.
7 Richard Dawkins, *The God Delusion* (London: Bantam Books, 2006).

8 For example, Simon Conway Morris in Cambridge.
9 For example, Keith Ward in Oxford.
10 See Sandro Magister, 'The Church and Islam: A Sprig of Dialogue has Sprouted in Regensburg', www.chiesa, 30 October
2006,
www.chiesa.espressonline.it?dettaglio.jsp?id=93245&eng=y
(accessed 15 January 2007).

3

Text and context: making sense of Islam in the modern world

ATAULLAH SIDDIQUI

Discussion of 'text', for Muslims, is discussion of the Qur'an. The exploration of the Qur'an – the Revelation – is central to the understanding of the *will of God* in Islam. The word of God was revealed to the Prophet Muhammad, an Arab, and therefore the text to be recited is in Arabic. In Islam, God chose a human agency to communicate with the people in a language they understood. The Qur'an in Islam is in fact tantamount to the importance of the person of Jesus for Christians. In Christianity the divine Logos becomes man, in Islam the divine logos – God's word – becomes text. Seyyed Hossein Nasr describes it in this way:

> The Word of God in Islam is the Qur'an; in Christianity it is Christ. The vehicle of the Divine Message in Christianity is the Virgin Mary; in Islam it is the soul of the Prophet. The Prophet must be unlettered for the same reason that the Virgin Mary must be virgin. The human vehicle of a Divine Message must be pure and untainted. The Divine Word can only be written on the pure and 'untouched' table of human receptivity. If this Word is in the form of flesh the purity is symbolized by the virginity of the mother who gives birth to the Word, and if it is in the form of a book this purity is symbolized by the unlettered nature of the person who is

chosen to announce this Word among men. One could not with any logic reject the unlettered nature of the Prophet and in the same breath defend the virginity of Mary. Both symbolize a profound aspect of this mystery of revelation and once understood one cannot be accepted and the other rejected.[1]

Just as it is important that the Prophet is unlettered, it is also important that he was of high moral standing, so that the received message could be applied honestly. A human Prophet was sent not only to communicate, but also to apply the teachings to himself first, and by showing this example encourage others to follow him and establish a universal Muslim community (*ummah*). As the Qur'an says, 'and We have revealed unto you [Muhammad] the Qur'an that you may explain to mankind that which has been revealed to them, and that haply they may reflect' (16:44).

The Revelation in Islam is eternal but its interpretation is not. Throughout the generations it has been interpreted and explained in the context in which people lived. Interpreters are human beings, and their thoughts and ideas are conditioned by the environment in which they live. Therefore there is no ultimate and final interpretation. Iranian scholar Abdolkarim Soroush describes it in this way:

This is not to desacrilize the sacred or to secularize religion, it is the simple and at the same time the subtle instance of naturalization of the supernatural, or if you like it better, the manifestation of the supernatural as and in the natural. The secular view is blind towards the supernatural, but here we look at the human interpretation as the revelation descended anew, from the heaven of the text to the earth of interpretation through the angel of reason, after its being revealed and descended to the prophet in the first place. In other words we look at the revelation through the interpretation, much the same as a faithful scientist who looks at the nature as an artifact of the creator. Of progress we are not certain, but evolution is certainly guaranteed. Now from this epistemological point of view, faith is seen to be the very commitment on the part of the faithful (believer) to take the word of God seriously and to interpret it sincerely and continuously, in order to gain general guidance for his life, both before and after death (this and the next life). This is what makes a believer distinct from the non-believer. Faith is always personal and private, it can be more or less certain, but knowledge cannot be but collective, public and fallible.[2]

The Qur'an should not simply be seen through an exegete's eye but it is also important to be aware of the fact that for Muslims it is a book of recitation and healing. The recitation of the Qur'an demands a continuous reading so that one must think, practise and heal again.

The Revelation and the human condition

After this brief introduction about the text/Qur'an I would like to explore how the Revelation relates to the human situation of the people. It is obvious that the Revelation does not function in a vacuum: it works within a context. It contains the multi-dimensionality of human relationships. I would like to highlight from the Qur'an three stories which show the relation-ship of the Revelation with God on the one hand and its relationship with people and with human conditions on the other.

The people of Madyan (Midian of the Bible) inhabited a territory which lay from the present-day Gulf of Aqaba west-ward into the Sinai Peninsula, which was later inhabited by the Arabs. They were situated at the crossroads of the trade routes from Yemen through Makka to Syria and from Iraq to Egypt. Madyan and its people were well known to the Arabs.

It was Midianite merchants to whom Joseph was sold into slavery. Their story and their prosperity, as well as their destruction, were part of the Arab memory. At the time of the Prophet Muhammad traders passed through the ruins of Madyan monuments.

Shu'ayb, identified by some with Jethro of the Old Testament, the father-in-law of Moses, was a Prophet who challenged his own people. Madyan society had five major social problems:

> (i) giving short measure or weight, whereas the strictest commercial probity is necessary for success, (ii) a more general form of such fraud, depriving people of rightful dues, (iii) producing mischief and disorder, whereas peace and order had been established . . . (iv) not content with upsetting settled life, taking to highway robbery . . . (v) cutting off people from access to the worship of God, and abusing religion and piety for crooked purposes . . . when a man builds a house of prayer out of unlawful gains or ostentatiously gives charity out of money which he has obtained by force or fraud, etc.[3]

The Qur'an describes Shu'ayb's plea to his people in this way:

> He said: 'O my people! Worship God alone: you have no deity other than Him. Clear evidence of the truth has now come unto you from your Sustainer. Give, therefore, full measure and weight [in all your dealings], and do not deprive people of what is rightfully theirs; and do not spread corruption on earth after it has been so well ordered: [all] this is for your own good, if you would but believe. And do not lie in ambush by every road [that leads to the truth], threatening and trying to turn away from God's path all who believe in Him, and trying to make it appear crooked. And remember [the time] when you were few, and [how] He

made you many: and behold what happened in the end to
the spreaders of corruption!'   (7:85–86)

While the story of Shu'ayb describes the general social corruption and his strong opposition to it, the following verse
in the same chapter provides another aspect of social evil:
the oppression and subjugation of a people. Enslavement
had deprived the children of Israel of all rights, and the
Pharaoh forced humiliation upon them simply because
they belonged to a different ethnic group. Pharaoh and the
Egyptians boasted of being descendants of a superior civilization and culture, and used their economic and military
might against the 'meek' people. The Qur'an describes the
situation in this way:

> And after those [early people] We sent Moses with Our
> messages unto Pharaoh and his great ones and they wilfully
> rejected them: and behold what happened in the end to
> those spreaders of corruption!
>
> And Moses said: 'O Pharaoh! Verily, I am an apostle from
> the Sustainer of all the worlds, so constituted that I cannot
> say anything about God but the truth. I have now come unto
> you with clear evidence from your Sustainer: let then, the
> children of Israel go with me!'   (7:103–105)

The struggle for freedom from oppressive regimes was the
major concern of Moses and his people. But the relevance of
the verse is eternal. This verse holds out hope for any similar
situation in human condition for the suppressed and warn-
ing for the oppressor.

The situation of Noah also provides an insight into how
the Revelation connects to a particular time and situation.
Noah says in the Qur'an, 'And behold, I called unto them
openly; and behold, I preached to them in public; and I
spoke to them secretly, in private and I said: Ask your

Sustainer to forgive you your sins – for, verily, He is all-forgiving.' If a community follows this path, then 'He will shower upon you heavenly blessings abundant, and will aid you with worldly goods and children, and will bestow upon you gardens, and bestow upon you running waters' (71:8–12). A good deed with good intention results in prosperity for people. The promise of paradise is not just something out there but it is also connected to this world as well. Recognizing human weaknesses, and that some people may act at times arrogantly, is important. But observing truthfulness and helping others, and above all asking forgiveness for human mistakes, are characteristics that the teachings of the prophets encourage us to discover and recognize.

The Qur'an's purpose is guidance, and the subject matter is obviously humanity whose welfare is paramount. What is also important to note is that the Prophet gave glad tidings, and warned people against the consequences of human actions on their personal and collective lives.

Interpreting the text in Islam

Prophet Muhammad was the first interpreter of the Qur'an and he established a community based on the qur'anic vision of society and values. That vision continues to shape society on the basis that the community should observe and encourage others to practise the *maruf* (known good), and oppose the opposite *munkar* (that which human nature instinctively loathes and rejects). This began a practice within the Muslim community of charting its path with sincerity and devotion, being true to the core values set by the Qur'an. But it also recognized the need to absorb and adapt according to time, context and space, with loyalty and without deviation. The mechanism is called *shariah* which means 'the path,' 'the way to the water'. As water symbolizes the source of life, so the *shariah* represents the source of Muslim existence. The basis of the *shariah* is the Qur'an, but it is also founded in the *sunnah*, the example of the Prophet Muhammad and how those norms and values were implemented in his lifetime. But the *shariah* actually only outlines some basic principles of norms and values. The rest is left to interpretation by those who are qualified and credible within the community.

But what are the objectives of the *shariah*? The objectives (*al-maqasid*) of the *shariah* and its implementation in a society, according to Al-Ghazali (d. 1111 CE), are 'to promote the welfare of the people, which lies in safeguarding their faith, their life, their intellect, their posterity and their wealth. Whatever ensures the safeguarding of these five serves the public interest and is desirable.' These aims were further enhanced by Ibn Tayimiyya (d. 1328) who added to the list things like the fulfilment of contracts, the preservation of ties of kinship and respect for the rights of one's neighbours. Essentially, he left this list open.[4] Ibn al-Qayyim (d. 1350) states that 'the basis of the Revelation and its understanding is wisdom and the welfare of the people in this world as well as in the Hereafter'. Welfare lies in complete justice, mercy, well-being and wisdom. Anything that departs from welfare to misery, or from wisdom to folly, has nothing to do with the Revelation and its objectives.

Fiqh is that method which has evolved in Islamic theology and jurisprudence in order to discern what is good and what is bad. The principles and objectives remain static, no matter how the details change to meet contemporary needs. The 'insight' and the 'comprehension' of the contemporary situation, and how that should be interpreted, is what we know as *fiqh*.

Muslims do not deal with some rigid, frozen entity called *shariah*, but with eternal values anchored in the Qur'an and the *sunnah* (the practice of the Prophet Muhammad), and developing as the human race progresses. Those who believe that the *shariah* is a fossilized entity are not aware of either the spirit of Islam or the needs of Muslim society.

Another point is worth clarifying at this juncture. Throughout the ages, Christian theology has developed according to the times and the contribution of various theologians who have made that possible. But it is largely the ecumenical councils which decided the nature of Christian theology. For example, the creed of Nicaea (325 CE) and the definitions of Chalcedon (451 CE) have had a lasting impact on churches all over the world. The need for such councils, and the need to arrive at decisions through mutual consultation and debate, are part of the Christian Church's make-up. The Muslim position and the development of Islamic thought have been far more individualistic and self-assertive, and furthermore fiercely independent. In Islamic history, people of intellect, integrity and vision have made their voices heard. Though they struggled and suffered from the persecution of rulers, nonetheless their voices were heard, if not in their own lifetimes, then later. In the absence of councils, Islamic thought was developed by various jurists and scholars.

However, the continuity of Muslim history and thought was disrupted. The institutions and mechanisms which were built to cope with the new challenges and evolve some new consensus were somehow demolished and upon them were superimposed institutions borrowed from the West, especially during the colonial period. Today, Muslim scholars are re-examining Muslim history and tradition, looking in depth at how far its flexibility will permit a change within

Islamic tradition. They are also examining how far western experiences and western models can be of help and could be accommodated in the contemporary Muslim ethical discourse. Muslims are cautious about accepting ideas of 'new theology' or 'new values' for the sake of it.

Muslim responses to modernity

The present situation is such that the decline of intellectual traditions, even before the European Enlightenment and later the impact of colonialism, has virtually created two tiers of educated Muslims. Muslim intellectual thought and western philosophical traditions went hand in hand in the medieval period; they understood each other clearly, to the extent that they quoted each other with ease. They were on the same wavelength, living in the same intellectual world and philosophical traditions; many writings in Islamic tradition influenced the West, and the western philosophical traditions influenced Islamic philosophy and thought. But gradually the intellectual and philosophical traditions declined, and philosophy came to be seen as something to disassociate from. It was seen as not being good science, and increasingly in Islamic religious schools philosophy was almost abandoned. Elementary logic was introduced as a subject, but philosophy as wider thought is missing even today, particularly in Sunni Islamic traditions.

Those who have studied in madrasas or seminaries have perhaps to a large extent been out of touch with developments in the fields of science, technology and other areas of philosophy and thought. Others who have studied within the 'modern' education system are practically unaware of the classical legacy of Islamic knowledge and in general the whole tradition of Islam. This situation has, however, forced

Muslims of both 'camps' to come together in search of meaning and values in the contemporary world. Therefore, on the one hand, educated Muslims – whether from seminaries or secular institutions – are not in a position to lead the community solely on the basis of their acquired knowledge. On the other hand, the individualist and self-assertive method of the previous generations is rapidly disappearing.

The colonial past created a great impact on the Muslim world. With the exception of two countries, Afghanistan and present-day Saudi Arabia, all Muslim countries were under the direct or indirect rule of the colonial empire. And what happened? The colonial masters were eager to produce clerks, not scholars. Because that was their immediate concern and need. During this period, in response to colonialism, three groups emerged.

The first, the *traditionalists*, rendered a great service to the Muslim community by preserving tradition, knowledge and experience, particularly at times when there was a danger of values being eroded. But, unfortunately, the traditionalists overemphasized preservation, which became their goal, and the challenge of recreation and transformation was often ignored. Engaging with the modern, ever-changing world was not the priority. They held the view that the challenge of colonialism was a temporary phase, and once it disappeared they would be able to return to the past with the preserved knowledge that they held so precious. Even after the independence of many Muslim countries, the traditionalists, largely the product of Muslim seminaries, are unengaged with the wider world and the challenges that they face today.

The second group, the *modernists*, tried to reinterpret Islam so that it seemed more appealing, rational and acceptable by modern standards. In their search for this 'new look', they largely ignored the role and importance of tradition in Islamic history and thought. Unfortunately, in the aftermath of the colonial period in many Muslim countries, leadership fell into the hands of those with modernist tendencies. They set about secularizing society even if they needed force to do so. Although the modernists were influenced by western values, they were very selective when it came to choosing which ones to implement. Rules and taxation were imposed upon people without their consent. In some parts of the Muslim world, monarchy was forced upon the population, in others military dictatorships were imposed. The economic exploitation, as well as the absence of freedom of expression and thought, created a tense and suspicious society.

Between these two trends emerged a third group, the *revivalists*. Under the umbrella of revivalism various trends and tendencies take shelter. This approach is seen as flexible, and, when compared with the previous two trends, there is a greater possibility of coming to terms with the modern world. However, their understanding of the western values that they confront is largely seen through political lenses, and the West is perceived as a monolithic Leviathan. Dialogue with the West here is largely non-existent.

The masses, unsatisfied with dictatorship, were looking for spiritual and religious solutions. Such sentiments were occasionally recognized by the military generals and dictators, and sometimes when they faced real difficulties these dictators opted for 'Islamic solutions' by declaring their fractured state to be an 'Islamic state'. They made sure that the façade was maintained by implementing harsh punishments and ignoring the plight of the poor and needy, and the general expectations of people to be able to express their views freely and choose their own representatives were pushed aside.

The Muslim community's search

In order to understand the situation of Islam and Muslims in the modern world further it would be helpful to divide the current Muslim situation into five phases. This will illustrate the development of the Muslim community and its search for its soul and identity. We will start with the mid-nineteenth century.

The *first* phase covers 1860 to 1924. For Muslims this was a period of transition. The overwhelming issues of the time were the colonial empires, the debate about new education and science, the preservation of orthodoxy, and the protection of the Ottoman Caliphate. The Deoband seminary and Aligarh Muslim University came into existence and represented the two tendencies of preservation and modernization in South Asia. Al-Azhar, the oldest and most prestigious seminary in Cairo, engendered a hot debate on modern education, particularly science. At the same time, the Turkish Caliphate came to an end and Turkey became a secular state. Secularism and modernization were imposed by force. In the Far East countries, such as Indonesia, the formation of a nationalist and political organization *Serikat Islam* (1912) and the emergence of the social and educational organization *Muhammadiyah* (1912) brought both national freedom and religious revival. Such activities throughout the Muslim world generated a vibrant debate on education, national identity and the place of Islam in the future building of nations.

The *second* phase was from 1924 to 1945. This period was dominated by colonial supremacy and influenced by western ideologies such as Nationalism and Socialism. The response to colonialism came in the form of Arab Nationalism. Western-educated Arabs transformed the political life of the

Arab world. Socialism made inroads too, and became increasingly popular. Parallel to these movements came the 'march of Islam'. Hassan al-Banna established the *Ikhwan al-Muslimun* (Muslim Brotherhood) in 1928 and Abul Ala Mawdudi the *Jamaat-e-Islami* in 1941. These two organizations presented Islam as a way of life, and suggested to the Muslim community that Muslims do not need any '-isms' – rather, the answers to all their problems lie in Islam and Islam alone. Al-Banna described his organization as 'a Salafi movement, a Sunni method, a Sufi reality, a political body, a sports group, a scientific and cultural league, an economic form and a social ideology'. Mawdudi, on the other hand, introduced the concept of the 'Islamic state' and presented a critique of western thought, including Communism. A reform movement, the *Tabligi Jamaat*, founded by Mawlana Ilyas, emerged from India and has influenced the international scene ever since. Nahdatul Ulama (1926) created the largest charitable organization in Indonesia and influenced the South East Asian religious scene over decades.

The *third* phase covers 1945 to 1979. This period saw intense activity and various experiments. The creation of Israel, refugees and mass migration to the West highlighted this intensity. At the same time, this was a period when Muslims established a number of national and international forums all over the world. International conferences addressed the crises of polity, economy and education, and Islamic law, science and technology. Muslims were re-examining their relationship with western thought and experiences vis-à-vis Islamic values. The greatest upheaval came in Iran where the Islamic Revolution succeeded in overthrowing the Shah and, by extension, diminishing American influence. With the occupation of Afghanistan, however, the influence of the Soviet Union increased, and a bloody, messy situation was created which even today we have not been able to resolve. Perhaps we could say that events in Iran were at the end of a long protest against one super-power, while events in Afghanistan were at the beginning of a protest against another.

The *fourth* phase runs from 1979 to 2001. The Gulf War, the Bosnian Crisis and the issue of *The Satanic Verses* (Salman Rushdie's book) dominated this period. The intense suspicion of western powers grew among Muslims. The issue of double standards and injustice was raised in relation to the Gulf War, Bosnia and, above all, Israel and its relationship with the United States. The year 1989 repre-sented a watershed in human history, particularly in the West and in the Muslim world. The fall of the Soviet Union unleashed massive historical forces that have rumbled ever since. The Berlin Wall that stood as the symbol of a divided western world was pulled down by the people. It not only resulted in redrawing the geographical map, but also the mental landscape of Europe. Many Muslim countries became independent, for example in Central Asia; however, their fate did not change. Democracy and freedom is still a far cry away.

The *fifth* phase begins with the 9/11 attack on America. The subsequent terrorist attacks in different parts of the world, including London in July 2005, have changed the dynamics of relations between Muslims outside and inside the western countries. The 'unruly' and 'ungrateful' inside, as perceived by some, and the 'barbarians' outside have been a predominant anxiety of governments and opinion-formers. The situation becomes even muddier since the attack on Afghanistan and the invasion of Iraq. Religious interpreta-tions are becoming more hardened towards the 'enemies' and 'infidels', and more and more solutions have been looked at from the examples of past confrontations that encouraged non-cooperation with those outside the Muslim community and mistrust of those Muslims who spoke differently. To suit the situation, meanings are increasingly being forced on the 'text'. One notices in this phase that the western powers are also capable of reversing their own stated policies of freedom and the rule of law against their own citizens. A deeper soul-searching is urgently required on both sides.

The five phases suggest the turmoil of the Muslim community, where there are anxieties about coming to terms with modernity and where the impact of colonialism is still felt throughout intellectual, social, political and economic thought. The opening up of the text in a new context seems not only a challenging task but also a risky one, where the temptation to accept the knowledge and experiences provided by modernity and the Enlightenment is enormous and ever present. Islamic knowledge and experiences need to be rediscovered and reconstructed.

We began our discussion with the Qur'an and its context and explored how it emphasizes the human condition, people's weaknesses and the danger of not heeding the message of the messengers. Today the text needs to be explored in a context where Muslims and those who are not Muslims are living side by side. The history of Muslims and their encounter with the western world (I do not see the West in a singular but plural sense; it is not monolithic) needs healing. The other dimension of the Qur'an needs to be discovered, that is, 'for those who believe it is Guidance and healing' (41:44). What the Qur'an demands from us is not simply a relationship with God but a deeper understanding of human conditions today, and it encourages us to establish a deeper relationship with fellow human beings marked by dignity and trust.

Differences of belief in Islam are seen as God's plan. The abolition of such differences is not the purpose of the Qur'an nor is the Prophet Muhammad sent for that purpose. The Qur'an also emphasizes that such differences do not suggest that their origin is different; rather it emphasizes that human beings have a common spirituality and morality (7:172; 91:7–10). These differences are there because God has given human beings the freedom to choose: 'And had your Lord so willed, all those who live on earth would have believed to faith altogether: would you force people against their will to believe!' (10:99). In this qur'anic vision of unity and diversity, the human task is to find a way to handle differences. In a society matters should be discussed, debated and a consensus should emerge, and no force should be allowed to countenance aggression and violence (22:39–40). In all these processes Muslims are bound by their belief to co-operate with all – Muslims or not – in securing peace and justice. Even if that justice points to the guilt of one's family – let alone the community – the Qur'an instructs that justice must prevail (4:135). It claims that for every community God has sent messengers and they will be 'judged between them with Justice, and they will not be wronged' (10:47). It also declares that for each community God has appointed a different path (*shariah*) and way (*minhaj*) (5:48). These different communities with various emphases of beliefs are encouraged to 'compete with one another (as in a race) in righteous deeds. Wherever you are God will bring you all together . . .' (2:148).

Today there is another message of the Messenger (the Prophet Muhammad), and not heeding to that message may bring the disaster which the people of earlier generations found themselves in. This time the danger is the literalist interpretation of text, without consideration for its spirit.

The Prophet said: 'There will come people of your faith, where prayers far surmount yours, and whose fasting far outdoes yours, their acts of worship are as large as mountains, yet they stray away from Islam as the arrow flees throughout the bow'.

Notes

1 S. H. Nasr, *Ideal and Realities of Islam* (London: Aquarian, 1966), pp. 43–4.
2 See 'Text in Context' lecture delivered at McGill University in April 1995, www.drsoroush.com.
3 See Abdullah Yusuf Ali, *The Holy Qur'an: Translation and Commentary* (Brentwood MD: Amana Corporation, 1983), p. 366, n. 1055.
4 See for details M. Hashim Kamali, '*Maqasid al-Shariah*: The Objectives of Islamic Law', *Newsletter* of the Association of Muslim Lawyers and the Islamic Foundation's Legal Studies Unit, 3/1 (April–June 1998), pp. 13–19.

4

Sacred text and the transcendence of tradition: the Bible in a pluralist society

FRANCES YOUNG

My title and subtitle break down into four themes: sacred scriptures in general; the Bible in particular; the transcendence of tradition; and our pluralist society. I shall explore each in turn here, though not in that order; I begin with the context in which we find ourselves.

Pluralist society

A Methodist theologian from Singapore, in a book published in 1990, wrote as follows:

> It is a pluralistic world. We can sing about the reality of pluralism. There is a variety of people and cultures. People are identified with race, religion, and nation. Cultures are distinguished by time periods and places in the world. Pluralism is unavoidable. This is a rainbow society.[1]

He suggests that in this situation 'we have a tendency to isolate ourselves' because we are more comfortable with those we know, those who are like us. He also observes that those who are powerful face the temptation to eradicate or dominate those who are different. A monolithic society discourages dissent; so pluralism is essential for a truly political society.

That is something brought home to me with some force in 1993, when I was involved in the World Faith and Order Conference in Santiago di Compostela. I shall never forget the session given over to Spanish Protestants to tell their story. Under Franco they had not been allowed to exist. This was a graphic reminder of the importance of the long battles for religious freedom which have taken place in European history. It was even a challenge to my long-held ecumenical hopes for a united Church: would not institutional unity be a recipe for religious totalitarianism? In the evening, however, the Roman Catholic Franciscans in Santiago lent their basilica to the Spanish Protestants, so that they could break bread with their brothers and sisters from across the globe. That ecclesiastical hospitality seemed a deeply significant sign of hope. Any monolithic society discourages dissent, and pluralism is indeed essential for a truly political society. But it requires respect for the 'other', even hospitality, rather than mere tolerance, let alone suppression!

Without pluralism there is no true democracy. But it demands that we break out of our isolation and engage in the public realm with those who are different. Retreat into mutually hostile camps, or the attempt to establish boundaries that are not porous, generates the partitions which have proved dubious ways of settling twentieth-century conflicts, creating oppressed minorities and even leading to ethnic cleansing. I think of Northern Ireland, the former Yugoslavia, Cyprus, Sri Lanka, Israel/Palestine. Lebanon and Iraq are examples of fractured societies without partition. Pluralist societies are not comfortable places to be, but they are better than ethnocentric enclaves, or an imposed uniformity.

In nearly all of the cases mentioned the situation has been compounded by differences in religion. The resurgence of religion in the former Soviet bloc has not helped to create pluralist societies in which differences are negotiated. I have been privileged to visit both Belgrade and Moscow. In Moscow the civic authorities have rebuilt in precise replica the cathedral put up to celebrate victory over Napoleon; Stalin had had it razed to the ground and replaced it by a swimming pool. The suppression of religion under communism has meant that its resurgence tends to create another monolithic society in which religion is annexed to nationalist identity. The same is true in Serbia. Religion has reinforced the desire to expunge difference – and so as elsewhere it has contributed to oppression and violence.

It is not surprising, then, that people increasingly perceive religion as a source of conflict. A *Guardian*/ICM poll at the end of 2006 showed that 82 per cent of respondents said that faith causes division and tension, though 57 per cent still think religion a force for good. Only 17 per cent regarded Britain as a Christian country; 62 per cent saw Britain as a religious country of many faiths. If pluralism is to be valued, then the faith traditions clearly need to find ways of negotiating with one another. That is, unless religion is just eliminated. According to another *Guardian* piece,

> People's fascination for religion and superstition will disappear within a few decades as television and the internet make it easier to get information, and scientists get closer to discovering a final theory of everything . . . Philosopher Daniel Denett (*sic*) believes that within 25 years religion will command little of the awe it seems to instil today. The spread of information . . . will 'gently, irresistibly, undermine the mindsets requisite for religious fanaticism and intolerance'.[2]

For a long time the leading academics and intellectuals in this country have tended to regard religion as passé, and the poll quoted above revealed that 15 per cent of respondents thought most people here do not believe in a god, and that only 33 per cent claim to be religious. All the subtle anti-religious trends in our society may ultimately be more effective in suppressing religion than the state atheism of the former Soviet Union. Certainly western Christianity seems increasingly weakened, and in Britain a far higher proportion of immigrants practise their religion than the indigenous population, as the same poll confirmed. But some of this is surely due to western consumerism and individualism. The postmodern assumption is that both modern science and the religions offer competing 'grand narratives' explaining life, the universe and everything – so you can choose between them, or be sceptical of them all and do your own thing. This has created a society in which the public realm is itself endangered. Politics, like religion, is overwhelmed by entertainment 24/7. Lack of commitment to anything and the primacy of choice exclude things, like relationships and religion, which require time and depth. Many have never given their children the opportunity to know what it means to be religious, imagining they can make their own choice when they grow up – religion has been privatized as a personal matter.

But faiths are not the kind of thing you can line up on a supermarket shelf. Most opinion-formers in our society clearly have no real knowledge or understanding of Christianity, or indeed of any other religious faith. In the new millennium, the apparent power of religion has caught commentators by surprise, and most movers and shakers are profoundly resistant to the idea that religion should have any role at all in the public sphere. So religious communities feel like oppressed minorities, as the monolithic secular society ridicules their beliefs and values. They become the more defensively aggressive and conservative in the face of this reality, retreating into the safety of their isolation while occasionally lashing out against trends in society they judge to be immoral. This is one of the factors in the rise of fundamentalisms, and precisely the opposite of what a pluralist society needs if it is to work effectively.

So to sum up this admittedly brief and inadequate survey: religion is perceived to be divisive; the majority are not religious; but a pluralist society is a public good; and for it to work it needs readiness to respect difference. Such is the context in which we are considering the place of sacred texts. It is a world in which people presume competition between the different sacred texts of different religious communities. It is a situation where the majority have little knowledge of any sacred text, where literary and artistic culture is barely touched by the Bible, despite its deep influence in this country over past centuries, and where there is no place for scriptures in the public realm, since politics and religion are supposed to be kept well apart. So there is a serious question whether any sacred texts could, or indeed should, have any influence at all on public life in general; and that question might seem exacerbated by the nature of sacred texts.

The nature of sacred texts

In the ancient world books seemed to defy mortality, allowing the absent authors of the past to speak in the present and impart wisdom for subsequent generations – they had an 'aura'. By contrast, in our society, books are two-a-penny (or two-for-one!) and some think they will soon be superseded by new technologies. While the past may be turned into a theme-park by the heritage industry, it is hardly regarded as offering much wisdom for our future, or change-oriented, culture. One reason why religions seem passé is their continued devotion to ancient books; in honouring particular books or collections of books, even giving them the status of holy objects, the major religions appear to live in the culture of antiquity rather than the (post)modern world.

Furthermore, as holy objects, the scriptures each belong to a particular religious tradition. Sacred texts are sacred because they are 'themselves' in the context of liturgy, prayer and worship. Let us consider a few snapshots. The story is told of a poor, illiterate Indian woman. She would spread out her prayer-mat, then take the Qur'an and hold it to her heart. 'She would then recall, crying like a child, that moment when the Voice repeatedly said to the Prophet in the cave of Hera: Read, Read in the Name of the Lord. And the Prophet had said in utter helplessness: I cannot read.' She would then go to the prayer-mat, lift the Qur'an above her head, and say, 'O Book! You are above my understanding. My head is nothing more than a place whereupon you rest.' Then, sitting on the prayer-mat, she would open the book, and follow the text with her finger, starting where she had left off the day before.

> What transpired between the book and that touch, and what knowledge passed, without any meditation or conscious thought, directly into her soul, only the Qur'an and that strange reciter could know. The entire world stood still at this amazing recital without words, without meaning, without knowledge. With that touch a unity was established between her and the Qur'an. At that moment she had passed into a state of total identity with the word of God.[3]

In a Buddhist monastery in Tibet, not so long ago, I watched monks, in their saffron robes, bent double, passing around three sides of their shrine, underneath huge cupboards which contained the Buddhist scriptures. They were literally and physically passing under their sacred texts, thus enacting their spiritual submission to the texts. The final snapshot is of Christian churches, in many of which the Gospel-book is processed, often with incense, before being read publicly. In Roman antiquity that is what people did with the images of the gods. Still in Mediterranean Catholic countries images of the Blessed Virgin Mary are processed at her festivals in this way. In Jewish synagogues the scrolls of Torah are likewise processed. Sacred texts stand in the place of sacred images as the mediators of the divine.

In every one of these cases it is not the content of the text that is directly in play. Rather, the physical object itself is venerated as holy, as mediating something that has an absolute claim over the worshipper. That is what a sacred text is. It is no ordinary book to read casually, like a novel, or even a work of philosophy.

An absolute claim that these texts are authoritative, at least for those who accept the claim, means there is a tendency for them to become fixed in form. In another Buddhist monastery in Tibet, I saw the ancient blocks from which the scriptures are printed. This block printing goes back centuries before the invention of printing in the West. Movable type has never been introduced for these scriptures. Every page is a separately carved block, carefully stacked in the right order from time immemorial. In a Jewish synagogue pride of place is given to the Ark of the Covenant, in which are stored the sacred scrolls, from which the Torah is read. The switch from scrolls to the book format took place in the third and fourth centuries of the Christian era. But in

Judaism, scrolls, written by hand, in Hebrew, remain the form of the text for liturgical purposes. The physical act of writing a new Torah is an act of deep religious meaning; every detail must be reproduced with absolute faithfulness and without error. Despite its diffusion across the globe, among many different ethnic and linguistic communities, the Qur'an is always recited in Arabic – strictly speaking it cannot be translated since translation is an act of interpretation. Some Muslims learn the whole Arabic text by heart: this oral transmission surely helps to guarantee the fixity of the text, for it is virtually impossible to modify a text that is lovingly cherished in the hearts of many. At the same time, the Qur'an itself speaks of the Lord teaching 'with the pen', and the writing down of the divine revelation in the Book means that calligraphy has been, and still is, one of the most valued of Islamic arts. Several traditional writing styles are used, but the text itself, they say, has been transcribed without alteration. Some anomalies in the text are supposed to go back to the Companions of the Prophet who memorized the original revelations, and they remain there because the text is unalterable.[4] Christianity might seem the exception that proves the rule. From the earliest times there have been versions of the scriptures in languages other than the original Greek of the New Testament and the Septuagint (Greek) version of the Old Testament: Syriac, Latin, Coptic, Armenian, Georgian, and so on. But the same tendency can be seen in the persistence of the Latin version in Roman Catholicism into the twentieth century, or Old Slavonic in the Russian Orthodox Church to this day, and the Authorized Version among some Evangelical and Pentecostal Christians.

But while the form of a sacred text remains unchanged, the very authoritative nature of the text generates debate about meaning. Exegesis is a contested area. In the same

Buddhist monastery where the scriptures were printed in the traditional way, I witnessed the ancient practice of dispute. In a particular spot, beside the main temple, at a set time, the monks would gather and pair off. One would set out a hypothesis; the other would listen and then respond with a contrary thesis. This would be accompanied with stamping and physical expressions of determined claims to be right. The very same week that Saddam Hussein's statue was torn to the ground in Baghdad, I was in Qatar, engaged in a conference with Muslim scholars, studying the Bible and the Qur'an side by side. It was the second 'Building Bridges Seminar' chaired by the Archbishop of Canterbury.[5] Much of the time was spent in small study groups. What impressed me was the way in which both Muslim and Christian scholars were able to say that some interpreters took a text this way, others understood it that way. Both communities were drawing on centuries of scholarly activity in which the exegesis of the sacred text was subject to debate, and reasoned arguments were advanced for understanding it one way or another.

Then again, because the text is authoritative, most religions have authorized interpreters to expound the text for those who have not spent time studying it, whether because they conduct the business of the world or because they are illiterate. When Jews, Christians or Muslims gather for worship, the text is not just read or recited, but there is a homily or sermon, expounding the text and applying it to the lives that the congregation live. For these sacred texts set out the right way of life for the believer who accepts their absolute claim. Not surprisingly, there are different interpretative traditions within each religion, different interpretative communities or, to use a Christian term, different denominations.

So the more one characterizes sacred texts, the more they seem bound by the communities that cherish them, and confined to their sacred locations, their rituals, their participating persons. Does not this captivity mean that sacred texts cannot possibly make any contribution to the public realm? The perception that it is the sacred texts which offer the competing and incompatible 'grand narratives' that contribute to the conflict of religions may seem confirmed. Their very antiquity, and the conservatism that traps them in ancient traditions, even ancient languages, surely disqualifies them from having any wider impact on a society that seeks innovation above all else, not to mention instant gratification, or at least immediate communication.

My argument so far would seem to point to profoundly negative conclusions. But hidden within it are seeds of hope, which I hope to draw out below. What I want to do is to uncover the implicit ways in which sacred texts point beyond themselves, and so to the possibility of the transcendence of tradition. As a Christian I shall explore the ways in which the Bible challenges us to engage with the 'other' with hospitality and respect. I shall refer to the work of progressive Muslims exploring the same agenda with respect to the Qur'an.[6] I shall suggest that each religious community has the potential to discover its own place in the rainbow society of pluralism if it becomes more responsive to its own sacred texts. So sacred texts will prove to have a crucial role in a pluralist society, which is far removed from the assumption that they are just competing and incompatible claims to truth. If allowed to, they can challenge and transform the outlook of their own adherents, so as to make them better citizens of a pluralist world. Furthermore, we can find within the various sacred texts common insights into the human condition, which can contribute to those values which permit a pluralist society to function. In pursuing this line of thinking I turn first to the Bible.

The Bible and its attitudes to the 'other'[7]

What Christians call the Old Testament may be described as the library of Jewish classics. It encompasses stories about national origins, religious and social laws, more than one version of early Jewish history, together with poetry and literature. It is therefore specific to a particular nation and its self-consciousness. There were originally twelve tribes of Israel in a confederation, whose common history included the Exodus from Egypt and the occupation of the Promised Land. By the time the scriptures were put together, ten tribes had been lost and only the Judaeans remained. By the time the New Testament came into being, the Jews were scattered all over the then known world, but retained their common identity, written as it was into their sacred literature.

A key element in their story is their election by 'the God of Abraham, Isaac and Jacob', who gave no name other than 'I am what I am' (or 'I will be what I will be'). This God entered into a covenant with them: 'If you obey my voice and keep my covenant, you shall be my treasured possession out of all the peoples' (Exodus 19.5). But it is also deeply written into these scriptures that this God is the God of all the earth. The very words just quoted continue: 'Indeed the whole earth is mine, but you shall be for me a priestly kingdom and a holy nation.' The chosen people have a role in the purposes of the one God of the whole world. So the Bible begins with God's act of creation. One might speak of a tension between universalism and particularity being written deep into what Christians call the Old Testament; alternatively one might discern in this the way that the universal God chooses to engage with the creation, namely through particularities.

The history of the chosen nation records warfare with 'others', with the expectation that God is on their side. Yet the notion of God's universal oversight had an impact on the nationalist tendencies of the biblical material. We may note the challenge offered by the prophets, who suggested that God's judgement on the people for not keeping the covenant would take the form of their conquest by the Assyrians, then the Babylonians. A generation or two after the capture of Jerusalem, the exiles in Babylon were told that God would now restore them to their land, and the agent would be Cyrus the Persian, who is even described (in Isaiah 45) as God's anointed one (= Messiah). Even those who do not know God may act on God's behalf.

In the Law revealed through Moses to the people, the stranger residing among the Israelites has a special place. Although not part of the covenant-people, the *gerim* (Hebrew for 'resident alien') should be treated with respect, protected against injustice and violence, and have the same privilege of rest on the Sabbath (Exodus 20.10; 23.12). 'A curse upon the one who withholds justice from the *gēr*, the orphan and the widow . . .' (Deuteronomy 27.19). Again like widows and orphans, the *gēr* has a right to the gleanings from grain, olive and grape harvests (Deuteronomy 24.19). The *gērim* are included in festivals, and were to be provided with food and clothing (Deuteronomy 16.11; 10.18). 'You shall not wrong a *gēr*, or be hard upon him; you were yourselves *gērim* in Egypt' (Exodus 22.21); 'You shall not oppress the *gēr* for you know how it feels to be a *gēr*; you were *gērim* yourselves in Egypt' (Exodus 23.9). The Israelite has the soul of the *gēr*, we might say. Key figures, such as Abraham and Elijah, are depicted as *gērim*. Even God appears as a *gēr* in

Jeremiah 14.8. So despite the nationalist focus of much of the material in the so-called Old Testament, there are features which encourage openness.

Furthermore, two books, Ruth and Jonah, specifically challenge exclusiveness. Ruth was the foreign daughter-in-law of an Israelite living abroad. The story tells of her determination to stay with her mother-in-law, Naomi, even when, after the death of her husband and two sons, Naomi decides to return to Israel. Ruth, the *gēr*, gleans the fields of a relative, who eventually takes her in marriage. There is no sign of embarrassment at the fact that the great King David was descended from this foreigner. However, exclusiveness clearly hardened in a later period, and the story of Jonah was the response. Jonah is the unwilling prophet who runs away from God's call. The call is to go to Nineveh, the capital city of the most powerful of Israel's enemies. Eventually Nineveh repents in response to his reluctant preaching, so God spares the city, and Jonah is completely put out! The book of Jonah appears among the books of the Twelve Prophets, but it is a strange book beside them: the foreign city, unlike Israel, repents when a prophet is sent; and God is merciful to foreigners, where Israel faced destruction as a result of God's judgement. It would seem to be more like a satire than a history. This seems to be confirmed by the extraordinary incident whereby Jonah is swallowed and regurgitated by a whale. A strong feature of the whole text is its affirmation of God's sovereignty over all of creation.

We could continue with exploration of the so-called 'wisdom' traditions in the Bible, texts which show deep connections with the general wisdom of the Ancient Near East and the Hellenistic world, but David Ford has already said something about wisdom in the Bible. So we turn to the New Testament. This presupposes the One God, Creator of all, and the story of this God's engagement with humanity through the chosen people of God, claiming that the Church is now the true people of God:

> You are the chosen race, the King's priests, the holy nation, God's own people, chosen to proclaim the wonderful acts of God, who called you out of darkness into his own marvellous light. At one time you were not God's people, but now you are his people; at one time you did not know God's mercy, but now you have received his mercy.
>
> (1 Peter 2.9–10, Good News Bible)

Such ideas were to have the legacy of supersessionism – the view that Christianity superseded Judaism. New boundaries were being established, even as old ones were challenged.

The question as to whether Jesus was a Jewish prophet, sent only to the lost sheep of the house of Israel (Matthew 15.24), or brought a revelation to non-Jewish peoples (the Gentiles), was one of the most contested issues in early Christianity, and the New Testament bears the marks of this argument. The earliest Christian documents we have are the Epistles of St Paul. Two of these at least (arguably more) are preoccupied with the questions raised by the conversion of non-Jews. Paul argues strongly that Gentiles should not be required to take on the ethnic marks of a Jew in order to become members of the believing community. He was clearly up against strong opponents who argued that salvation through Christ presupposed being a loyal Jew, and therefore the Jewish identity-markers of circumcision and keeping Torah should be required, just as if they were proselytes to Judaism. So, on the one hand, the mission to Gentiles implies that the gospel is universal and not confined to Jews; on the other hand it encourages a strong differentiation between those who accept the gospel message and become believers and those, whether Jews or Gentiles, who do not. Nevertheless, for the Pauline tradition, it is really important that a new humanity has been forged in Christ in which the old divisions between Jews and Gentiles have been healed and transformed.

Jesus himself, a Jew in a Jewish society, is depicted in the Gospels as breaking across boundaries – a brief catalogue would include the following: the core commandments of Jesus are to love God and love our neighbours – indeed, even to love our enemies. Jesus clearly welcomed people who were marginalized in his society, such as women, children, even lepers and some who were regarded as sinners by the religious leaders of the time. He told parables about welcoming outsiders to the feast of the Kingdom. Many stories indicate the openness of Jesus to people usually treated with suspicion because they were non-Jews: for example, the parable of the good Samaritan, or healing the servant of the Roman centurion – a Gentile. Jesus told people not to judge others, in case they were judged by God. Jesus told his disciples not to stop someone driving out demons in his name, even though he did not belong to the group of the disciples, because 'whoever is not against you is for you'. According to some versions of the story Jesus 'cleansed the temple' for the sake of Gentiles, protesting, 'It is written in the scriptures that God said, "My temple will be called a house of prayer for the people of all nations". But you have turned it into a den of thieves' (Matthew 21.13; Mark 11.17; Luke 19.46). In the Gospel of John, however, there is one definitive verse which, for many Christian believers, indicates that only through Christ is salvation possible. According to John 14.6, Jesus said, 'I am the way, the truth and the life; no one comes to the Father but by me.' Many Christians simply take the statement at face value as the authoritative word of Jesus, but maybe a different perspective results from setting it in context. The statement appears in the so-called 'farewell discourses'. Here Jesus is presented as speaking to the disciples alone, that is, to those who will recognize him as coming from the Father, and later on, when the Spirit has led them into all truth, will understand the message of the gospel as a whole, namely, that he is the Logos/Word of God, an idea explored at the very beginning of the Gospel.

The opening words of the prologue of John's Gospel assert that God was 'in the beginning', picking up the very first words of the Bible (Genesis 1.1). The biblical claim about the one true God, who is the Creator of all that is, thus provides the fundamental perspective. The Word is with God, indeed is God – for it was through him that everything was made. Life is in him, and life is light for humankind. Of course, this universal, divine Word is the way, the truth and the life, for all human creatures. According to the prologue, however, the light shone in the darkness, and the darkness could not grasp it. The true light enlightens everybody. It was in the world, and the world came into being through it, but the world didn't recognize it. In this way the prologue sketches the drama of the story to follow. The Word of the Lord came to prophets, who were rejected. The Word of the Lord came in person, and was rejected. God's wisdom may be universal, but it is also contested. The prologue thus grapples with the tension between the particular manifestation of the Word in Jesus Christ and the universal presence of God's Wisdom in all creation. Jesus is not the exclusive presence of the Logos, rather the full embodiment of that Word which was already present in the prophets, and in all wise men and women of every culture. In the second century, Christian apologists, such as Justin Martyr, would claim that Jesus was the fulfilment of both prophecy and philosophy – affirming the presence of the Logos in Socrates as well as Isaiah. Christ is the way, the truth and life to which all philosophy, all religion, points.

The Bible encourages believers to find their identity and the meaning of their lives in its overarching story; but it also challenges them to recognize that their God is the God of the whole universe, and that they cannot confine God to their own community – indeed, the challenge is to perceive, in all humility, that God has always been at work among those who are outside the boundaries of the community. Within the Christian community the interpretation of the Bible is contested. Yet surely history has shown that in new situations new meanings may be discerned: slavery was once thought to be endorsed by the Bible, but hardly any more. Pluralism requires those of us who honour the Bible to explore its dynamics with these new questions, and discover its potential to hold together, on the one hand, the truths that make believers free and, on the other, the wider perspective that encourages believers to engage fruitfully with those who are different, to confront narrow fundamentalisms and transcend their traditions.

The transcendence of tradition

Christians are not alone in engaging in that process. You may recall the publication of Jonathan Sacks' book, *The Dignity of Difference*;[8] which caused great controversy within his own community, as is typical for such prophetic voices. The Chief Rabbi showed us all the value of pluralism, building his case from the Hebrew Bible. Within Islam, too, there is the same kind of development:

At the heart of a progressive Muslim interpretation is a simple yet radical idea: every human life, female and male, Muslim and non-Muslim, rich or poor, 'Northern' or 'Southern', has exactly the same intrinsic worth . . . because, as the Qur'an reminds us, each of us has the breath of God who breathed into our being.[9]

It is the Qur'an, 'not some contemporary ideology such as Marxism', which drives progressive Muslims:

Ours is a relentless effort to submit the human will to the Divine in a way that affirms the common humanity of all God's creation. We conceive of a way of being Muslim that engages and affirms the humanity of all human beings, that actively holds all of us responsible for a fair and just distribution of God-given natural resources, and that seeks to live in harmony with the natural world.

Serious engagement with the textual resources of the Islamic tradition is vital for this project, they insist.[10] Otherwise this is just giving an 'Islamic veneer' to 'programs for social reform [which] could just as easily come from Christian, Jewish, Hindu, Buddhist, Secular Humanist, or agnostic progressives'. They insist that human rights may be 'derived from the Qur'an and the Sunnah [the way of the Prophet]', which 'lend themselves to arguments favoring democratic forms of governments, pluralistic societies and schemes of human rights'.[11] From this base they not only challenge the arrogance of modernity, evident in current US foreign policy, but also expose the failure of Muslim societies to create the justice and pluralism implicit in the Qur'an. They even insist that when confronted by contemporary tragedies, whether in Bosnia, Palestine, Gujarat or Kashmir, Muslims should be as concerned for non-Muslims as they are for fellow believers.[12]

Many have drawn our attention to the positive statements made about Jews and Christians in the Qur'an, and told traditional stories of how the 'people of the Book' were welcomed and embraced by Muhammad, despite the critique of Jews and Christians also offered in the scriptures and traditions of Islam.[13] There is a tension between inclusiveness and exclusiveness here, not dissimilar to that traced in the Bible. In Islam too, then, the interpretation of the sacred text is contested. Yet there are those who point to the ways in which tradition may be transcended.

Within Christianity, two things, one ancient and one recent, may provide a double foundation for building transcendence of tradition. The recent development is found in an important shift in the approach to interpretation. Throughout the nineteenth and twentieth centuries arguments about the Bible tended to be focused particularly on the original or historical meaning, or on the facts behind the text. In our postmodern world, however, the focus has shifted, from the past to the future of the text. The admittedly contested implications of the text for current moral questions, such as homosexuality, abortion, euthanasia, even the ordination of women, have a more vital and immediate resonance than the 'quest for the historical Jesus', old or new. Modernity differentiated between the culture of the present and that of the past in which the scriptures were composed; now these postmodern questions demand that we explore how one might distinguish culturally conditioned aspects of the text and the core thrust of what the Bible is about. There is a sense in which I have already exemplified that procedure in exploring the Bible and its attitudes to the 'other'.

But I mentioned a double foundation for building transcendence of tradition; the ancient element is in deeply traditional theological perspectives, too easily overlooked.

'My thoughts are not your thoughts, neither are your ways my ways, says the Lord. For as the heavens are higher than the earth, so are my ways higher than your ways and my thoughts than your thoughts' (Isaiah 55.8–9). This was a favourite text among the church fathers who insisted that God's essence is beyond our understanding, especially against those heretics who wanted to define God rather too precisely; if you can define the infinite God you have set boundaries around divinity and reduced God to the size of your own mind, they insisted. The only reason we know anything about God is because God has accommodated the divine self to our level, not only in what Christians call the incarnation, but also by clothing the divine Word in human words, by using metaphors and symbols that point beyond themselves to the divine. Religious language is always human language stretched to express things beyond our comprehension, dimly perceived through analogy, and only partially understood.

All revelation, then, is culturally conditioned. Interpretation constantly has to wrestle with the tension between the particularity of sacred texts and the universal perspective implicit in them. The mode of divine mediation seems to be particularity, as God addresses particular people in particular situations; perhaps we too easily absolutize the particulars through which the mediation occurs. With this overarching perspective Christians may wish to embrace in their own way two well-known parables from the East, where different religious traditions have lived, for the most part peacefully, side by side for centuries: first, the story of the blind men and the elephant, one blind man feeling the tail and suggesting an elephant is a bell-pull, another feeling a leg and suggesting it is a tree, another feeling the trunk and deciding it is a hose-pipe; second, the picture of a mountain, and people going up by different paths on different sides of the mountain, and so seeing different views, and indeed seeing the mountain differently, but it is the same mountain. Both stories imply a certain relativism, but they also presuppose that there is a single reality which is actually perceived differently by the different witnesses. The relativism of limited creatures is another way of expressing humility before the transcendent divine.

A Turkish scholar, Fethullah Gulen, once wrote:

> Regardless of how their adherents implement their faith in their daily lives, such generally accepted values as love, respect, tolerance, forgiveness, mercy, human rights, peace, brotherhood, and freedom are all values exalted by religion. Most of these values are accorded the highest precedence in the messages brought by Moses, Jesus, and Muhammad, upon them be peace, as well as in the messages of Buddha and even Zarathustra, Lao-Tzu, Confucius, and the Hindu prophets.[14]

It is extremely important that such words come from the non-western world, because in our post-colonial world it is too easy, when appeal is made to universal values, for westerners to be heard as imposing their values on others. Indeed, the listing of such values may, of course, conceal very different connotations in different cultures. Yet we need the kind of dialogue that both reveals and refines such common ideals. They are essential for our pluralist world.

We need more than mere tolerance, which implies each group keeping themselves to themselves and not causing trouble! We should note three points.[15] First, pluralism is not simply the same thing as diversity. One may have people from different religious and ethnic backgrounds present in one place, but unless they are involved in an active engagement with one another, there is no pluralism. In other words, pluralism is not and cannot be a non-participant sport. Second, the goal of pluralism is not simply 'tolerance' of the other, but rather an active attempt to arrive at an understanding. The very language of tolerance in fact keeps us from the kind of engagement we are speaking of here. One can tolerate a neighbour about whom one remains thoroughly ignorant. That stance, while no doubt preferable to outright conflict, is still far from genuine pluralism. Third, pluralism is not the same thing as relativism. Far from simply ignoring the profound differences among religious traditions, a genuine pluralistic perspective would be committed to engaging the very differences that we have considered, to gain a deeper sense of each other's commitments.

What I have just quoted is a Muslim's summary of points made in a book called *A New Religious America: How a Christian Country Has Now Become the World's Most Religiously Diverse Nation*.[16] As we in Britain grapple with similar developments, let us recognize that our sacred texts, which could so easily cement our mutual isolation, might in fact become the greatest resource for mutual engagement and a discovery of common values which could contribute to the proper pluralism of the public realm. Let the Chief Rabbi have the final word:

> Pluralism is a form of hope, because it is founded in the understanding that precisely because we are different, each of us has something unique to contribute to the shared project of which we are a part . . . There are multiple universes of wisdom, each capturing something of the radiance of being and refracting it into the lives of its followers, none refuting or excluding the others, each as it were the native language of its followers, but combining in a hymn of glory to the creator.[17]

Notes

1 Yap Kim Hao, *Doing Theology in a Pluralistic World* (Singapore: The Methodist Book Room, 1990).
2 Report by Alok Jha (science correspondent), 'No religion and an end to war: how thinkers see the future', *Guardian*, 1 January 2007.
3 Hasan Askari, *Alone to Alone: From Awareness to Vision* (Leeds: Seven Mirrors, 1991), p. 113; quoted by Tim Winter in Michael Ipgrave (ed.), *Scriptures in Dialogue: Christians and Muslims Studying the Bible and Qur'ān Together* (London: Church House Publishing, 2004), pp. 51–2.
4 Sayyid Siddiq Hasan, *Reflections on the Collection of the Qur'ān*, trans. A. R. Kidwai (Birmingham: Qur'ānic Arabic Foundation, 1999).
5 The proceedings were published in Ipgrave (ed.), *Scriptures in Dialogue*.
6 Omid Safi (ed.), *Progressive Muslims on Justice, Gender, and Pluralism* (Oxford: Oneworld Publications, 2003); *The Muslim World*, an academic journal published by Hartford Seminary, Connecticut, since 1911, particularly a special issue devoted to the contributions of a Turkish thinker, Fethullah Gulen, vol. 95.3 (July 2005).
7 In this section I have here borrowed from and adapted the lecture I gave in Qatar, published in Ipgrave (ed.), *Scriptures in Dialogue*.
8 Jonathan Sacks, *The Dignity of Difference: How to Avoid the Clash of Civilizations* (London: Continuum, 2002).
9 Safi (ed.), *Progressive Muslims*, p. 3.
10 Safi (ed.), *Progressive Muslims*, p. 7.
11 Safi (ed.), *Progressive Muslims*, p. 292.
12 Safi (ed.), *Progressive Muslims*, p. 329; cf. *The Muslim World*, vol. 95.3 (July 2005), p. 449.
13 Safi (ed.), *Progressive Muslims*, pp. 252–5; Ipgrave (ed.), *Scriptures in Dialogue*, pp. 115–18.
14 *The Muslim World*, vol. 95.3 (July 2005), p. 376.
15 Safi (ed.), *Progressive Muslims*, p. 252.

16 Diana Eck, *A New Religious America: How a Christian Country Has Now Become the World's Most Religiously Diverse Nation* (San Francisco: HarperSanFrancisco, 2001).

17 Sacks, *The Dignity of Difference*, pp. 203, 204.

5

The Bible and the Middle East

DAN COHN-SHERBOK

Liberating Texts? is designed to address public issues on the basis of sacred texts. I have chosen to focus on the Hebrew Bible and the Middle East. Given this subject, you might expect me to illustrate how the Bible can be used to foster peace between Jews and Palestinians. Indeed, many years ago when I was a congregational rabbi I did just this in my sermons. On one occasion – in Jasper, Alabama, where I was a student rabbi – I cited a messianic passage from Isaiah to demonstrate the desirability of peace in the Holy Land:

> It shall come to pass in the latter days
>> that the mountain of the house of the LORD shall be
>>> established as the highest of the mountains,
>> and shall be raised above the hills;
> and all nations shall flow to it,
>> and many peoples shall come and say:
> 'Come, let us go up to the mountain of the LORD'
> . . .
> He shall judge between the nations,
>> and shall decide for many peoples;
> and they shall beat their swords into ploughshares,
>> and their spears into pruning hooks;
> nation shall not lift up sword against nation,
>> neither shall they learn war any more.
>
>> (Isaiah 2.2–4, RSV)

I remember one of the congregation was exceedingly annoyed with me because I did not champion the Jewish cause. He walked out of the synagogue and vowed never to return. He would have been much happier if I had used the Bible to demonstrate that Israel has a divine right to the land.

Of course, I could have done that. Let me give you an example of what I might have said. In the Book of Joshua, the Israelites were commanded to take the land away from the Canaanites. In the first chapter of Joshua, we read:

> After the death of Moses, the servant of the LORD, the LORD said to Joshua, the son of Nun, Moses' minister, 'Moses my servant is dead; now therefore rise, go over this Jordan, you and all this people, into the land which I am giving to them, to the people of Israel. Every place that the sole of your foot will tread upon I have given to you, as I promised to Moses. (Joshua 1.1–3, RSV)

In the Judaism course that I teach at the University of Wales (Lampeter), I cite this and other passages from the Book of Joshua, where the Canaanites were slaughtered by the ancient Israelites. I ask my students: if the Bible justifies such a massacre in the eleventh century BCE, would not the Israelis today be justified in driving out the Palestinians? Not surprisingly, when posed with this question some of my students – particularly those of a more evangelical disposition – become uncomfortable. They believe the Bible is true; that it is the word of God. But they cannot reconcile this narrative of conquest and destruction with their belief in a compassionate and caring God. And they certainly do not wish to see the Bible used as a basis for crushing Palestinian aspirations.

The difficulty is that the Bible is not a monolithic text. It is a work of many hands, with a variety of different views.

And, if you think about it, it is obvious that there is simply no way of isolating the core elements and utilizing them in a systematic fashion. Rather, the Bible contains differing and conflicting opinions about a wide range of issues. Obviously this has not restrained interpreters from grounding their views on biblical texts. All preachers do it. But, we do need to recognize that the selection of one text over another is a matter of subjective preference. The Bible speaks with many voices – it is a cacophony of voices. And there is a danger – a very great danger – in assuming that scripture speaks uniformly and consistently.

Use of the Bible by Christian Zionists

That has been the mistake of one increasingly large group of Christians today who have based their understanding of the Middle East conflict on the Hebrew Bible. These Christian Zionists are convinced that the Old Testament provides a framework for understanding the role of the Jewish people in God's providential plan. I should emphasize that the Christian Zionist lobby is not a tiny, marginal group within the Christian community. There are millions of Christian Zionists who believe that their understanding of Middle East events is grounded in God's will. This is how they are described by Dale Crowley in Grace Halsell's study of Christian Zionism, *Forcing God's Hand*:

> There's a new religious cult in America. It's not composed of so-called 'crazies' so much as the mainstream, middle-to-upper-middle-class Americans. They listen – and give millions of dollars each week – to the TV evangelists who expound the fundamentals of the cult. They read Hal Lindsey and Tim LaHaye. They have one goal: to facilitate God's hand to waft them up to heaven free from all trouble,

from where they will watch Armageddon and the destruction of Planet Earth. The doctrine pervades Assemblies of
God, Pentecostal, and other charismatic churches, as well as
Southern Baptist, independent Baptist, and countless so-
called Bible churches and megachurches. At least one out of
every ten Americans is a devoted member of this cult. It is
the fastest growing religious movement in Christianity
today.[1]

This is rather scary, isn't it? But Christian Zionism is not a
new phenomenon. For centuries a number of influential
Christian thinkers insisted that the Jewish people must
return to the Holy Land prior to the Second Coming. Let me
take you back to the seventeenth century. In 1649 two English
Puritans, Johanna and her son Ebenezer Cartwright, called
for the repeal of the Act of Parliament that banished Jews
from England. By reading the Bible in English, they learned
that Palestine was the ancestral home of the Jews and the
goal of the divinely promised return. The Kingdom of God
on earth was for all nations, they believed, and this would
occur when the people of Israel were restored to Jerusalem.
The Bible served as the foundation of their belief. And note:
these early Christian Zionists were not principally interested
in the fate of the Jewish nation. Their desire to see the
restoration of the Jewish people grew out of a longing for
Jesus' return. It was not the Jews themselves who mattered,
but Christ's millennial kingdom.

Another striking example of early Christian Zionism was
the eighteenth-century theologian Dr Thomas Burnet, who
was convinced that the Jewish people will have a special role
in the kingdom of the Messiah. In his view, the time for the
promised restitution of the Jews was bound to arrive, and
then the Jews would revive again in the land of their forefathers. There is no promise more often repeated in scripture,

he declared, than that which concerns the preservation and future restoration of the Jews.

For contemporary Christian Zionists, the most important early thinker was John Nelson Darby, who was influenced by Edward Irving. In 1826 Irving translated a work by Manuel Lacunza, a Spanish Jesuit, entitled *The Coming of the Messiah in Glory and Majesty*. To this work, Irving added a 203-page preface in which he gave his own prophetic speculations about the end of the world, predicting the apostasy of Christendom, the eventual restoration of the Jews and the imminent return of Christ. Irving's views had a profound impact on Darby. Ordained in the Church of Ireland in 1825, Darby taught that the promises made to the Jewish people were unfulfilled and would find their eventual consummation in the reign of Jesus Christ on earth during the millennium. For Darby, the Jews will serve as the primary instrument of God's rule during the millennium. The Lord will empty the land of its inhabitants and give it to Israel. Then, he believed, the Jews will rule on earth in league with Satan. In this regard, he formulated two stages in Christ's return. First, Christians would meet Christ in the air and be 'raptured' from the earth. Then the Antichrist would arise. His rule would finally be destroyed by the appearance of Christ on earth.

Due to Darby's tours of the United States, his ideas gained a wide audience. Those influenced by Darby included such Christian leaders as William Blackstone and C. I. Scofield whose Scofield Bible had a major influence on evangelical thought. In Scofield's view, the church age will end in failure and apostasy and be replaced by a revived national Israel who will experience the blessings of the final kingdom dispensation. Following Darby, Scofield maintained that God has a separate plan for Israel and another for the Church.

Israel's destiny is on earth while the Church's is in heaven. During the great Tribulation on earth a remnant of Israel will turn to Jesus as the Messiah and become his witness. Scofield's Bible had a major influence in the years following its publication. By 1945 more than two million copies had been published in the United States; between 1967 and 1979 a further one million copies of the New Scofield Reference Bible appeared; and in 1984 a new edition was published.

In time other Christian Zionists championed this interpretation of history known as dispensationalism. More recently dispensationalism has been popularized by such writers as Hal Lindsey, whose books portrayed the period of Tribulation in graphic terms. Like others before him, Lindsey argued that the Bible foretells the future. In his most famous work, *The Late Great Planet Earth* (1970), he depicts the dangers facing humanity. In his view, the battle of Armageddon is unavoidable. Only by believing in Jesus can the faithful be saved and avoid a global holocaust. In presenting his predictions, Lindsey is sympathetic to Israel, stressing that the promises made to Abraham are eternal.

For Lindsey, God will not forsake the Jewish people, and all nations will receive blessings through Israel. Biblical prophecy demands national restoration of the Jewish people. However, in his view, many Israelis will die in the holocaust of Armageddon, but the Church will be replaced by Israel as the people of God on earth. Within this framework, Lindsey maintains that the incorporation of the Occupied Territories into Israel is essential. Further, the occupation of Jerusalem must also continue, since it will become the spiritual centre of all the world. All peoples will come to worship Jesus there, and he will rule from the holy city. In *The Late Great Planet Earth*, Lindsey describes Armageddon;

although he insists that Christians who embrace a dispensational theology will be 'raptured' before the Tribulation commences.

This picture of the final days is graphically portrayed in the series of novels written by Tim LaHaye and Jerry B. Jenkins. Along with Lindsey, LaHaye has become a successful popularizer of dispensationalism. Implicit in his works is a fatalistic view of the future. LaHaye's mission has been to gain support for the political agenda of the religious right. His *Left Behind* series reinforces the fear that there is a sinister group at work creating a one-world socialist gulag for those who have not been saved. According to LaHaye his novels are true to the literal interpretation of biblical prophecy.

Beginning with *Left Behind: A Novel of the Earth's Last Days* (1995), the series depicts the period of Tribulation and the final Armageddon. In the first novel in the series, passengers aboard a Boeing 747 en route to Europe disappear instantly. Nothing remains except the passengers' crumpled piles of clothes, jewellery, fillings and surgical pins. Vehicles, suddenly unmanned, career out of control. People are terror-stricken as loved ones vanish before their eyes. This is the period of Rapture. The novels which follow describe the time of Tribulation. In the penultimate novel, *Glorious Appearing* (2004), believers look to heaven for the appearance of Christ, who will return and rule over all the world. The Tribulation Force has migrated to the Middle East. Jerusalem is falling to the global community's Unity Army and Tsion ben-Judah has been slain. It is now over seven years since the Rapture and almost seven years since Antichrist's covenant with Israel. Believers look to the heavens for the glorious appearance of Christ. All appears doomed, but God has another plan.

The impact of Christian Zionism in Middle Eastern affairs

Now, you might think that these writers have had little influence on American life. This is a mistake. Literally millions of copies have sold to a profoundly religious audience. Simultaneously, leading evangelicals, including Jerry Falwell and Pat Robertson, have had a profound influence on American Christian evangelism. After the Six-Day War, Falwell became an ardent supporter of the Jewish state. Like other evangelical Americans, he gave full support to Israel's victory over Arab forces. In response, the State of Israel gave Falwell a Lear jet to help him in his work to encourage others to support a Jewish presence in the Holy Land. Together with Jerry Falwell, Pat Robertson is one of the most important Christian supporters of Israel in the United States. His Christian Broadcasting Network was the first and remains the most influential Christian satellite TV network in the world.

Most significantly, in the political sphere, Christian Zionists have also come to occupy a central role. By the 1980s Christian Zionism began to influence American policy. About 20 million fundamentalist and evangelical Christians voted for Ronald Reagan, who was an ardent supporter of Israel. As a consequence, pro-Israel Republicans gained a stronghold in the government. On at least seven public occasions President Reagan expressed his belief in a final battle of Armageddon. At White House seminars organized by the administration and the Christian right along with the pro-Israel lobby, Christian Zionists, including Hal Lindsey, Jerry Falwell and Pat Robertson, expressed their support for the Jewish state.

In Israel itself, Benjamin Netanyahu became a favourite of the Christian Zionists; he spoke frequently at Christian Zionists' functions, including the Feast of Tabernacles hosted by the International Christian Embassy in Jerusalem. Within a few months of his election as Prime Minister in May 1996, Netanyahu convened the Christian Advocacy Council, bringing 17 American fundamentalist leaders to Israel. This tour concluded with a conference and a statement in line with the right-wing Israeli party Likud's political policy. On their return to the United States, Christian Zionist leaders launched a national campaign with full-page advertisements in major newspapers under the banner: 'Christians call for a united Jerusalem'. Likud also sought Christian Zionist help in offsetting the decline in contributions to Israel from American Jews. As a result, the International Fellowship of Christians and Jews raised over five million dollars, largely from fundamentalist Christians. Later, Christian Zionists worked with pro-Israel groups to mobilize constituencies to make telephone calls and send emails and letters to President Bush, encouraging him to stop putting pressure on Prime Minister Ariel Sharon to withdraw his forces from Palestine areas.

Christian Zionist organizations and the pro-Israel lobby are among the special-interest groups whose concerns have converged since George W. Bush was first elected president. These interest groups include the right wing of the Republican Party; neo-Conservatives; multinational construction firms, the petroleum industry and the arms industry; the pro-Israel lobby and think-tanks; and fundamentalist Zionist Christians. During the last 20 years, the conservative evangelical movement has been the fastest growing sector within American Christian circles.

Estimates of the number of evangelicals range from 100 million to 130 million. Most of these individuals are inclined to support the Christian Zionist position. A recent poll by the Pew Research Centre, for example, noted that 58 per cent of evangelicals believe in the battle of Armageddon. Today, these Christian Zionists constitute the largest base support for pro-Israel interests in the United States. Not surprisingly, these vast numbers of Christian supporters of Israel have adopted a highly critical attitude towards the Arab world. With the emergence of Arab nationalism and the growing aspirations of Palestinians, the polemic against Arabs has intensified. A typical example is Jan van der Hoeven of the International Christian Embassy in Jerusalem. Castigating Arab attitudes, he wrote:

> The greatest hero (in the Arab world) is Hitler. Hitler's *Mein Kampf* is still required reading in various Arab capitals and universities . . . The only reason that the Arabs have not yet done to the Israeli Jews what Hitler did to their forefathers in Europe is that they have thus far lacked the military means and weapons of mass destruction which were at Hitler's disposal to do so. Had there not been an Israeli Defense Force to defend the remnant of European Jewry that immigrated to Israel, the Arabs would have gladly fulfilled Hitler's dream a long time ago by finishing off those of the Jews the Nazi megalomaniac had left alive.[2]

Similarly, Hal Lindsey denounced the Arab world for its offensive against Israel: 'Long ago the psalmist predicted the final mad attempt of the confederated Arab armies to destroy the nation of Israel. The Palestinians are determined to trouble the world until they repossess what they feel is their land.'[3]

Frequently Islam is also demonized, particularly after the events of September 11, 2001. Various Christian Zionist writers have described America's war against Islamic terrorism following this event. Hal Lindsey's writings, for example, are characterized by Arab negative stereotypes:

> All Muslims see Israel as their enemy . . . The Arab nations are united in their fanatical obsession to destroy Israel . . . Agreements in the Arab nations don't mean the same thing they mean in the Judeo-Christian world. Islam not only has a track record of re-interpreting, denouncing and reversing settlements, such actions are actually encouraged if they further the cause of Allah . . . The movement seeks not only to destroy the State of Israel but also the overthrow of the Judeo-Christian culture – the very foundation of western civilization . . . They have, like the Communists, at their philosophic core the sworn duty to 'bury us'.[4]

According to some Christian Zionists, those who support the Arab world against Israel are acting against God. As David Brickner cautioned:

> Peril awaits those who presume to say that God is finished with his chosen people . . . Just as God judged the nation of Egypt for all her ill treatment of His people, so will He judge nations today. Evangelicals who would understand the Middle East must pay close attention to the teaching of Scripture, and take note of the cosmic forces that now do battle in the heavens but will soon do battle on earth.[5]

I have quoted these passages at some length to demonstrate the fanatical attitude of modern Christian Zionists regarding the State of Israel and the world of Islam. While demonizing Islam, Christian Zionists have sanctioned the relationship between Israel and the United States. Continually they take the side of Israel in its negotiations with the Arab world, recognizing that they share a common war against Islamic terrorism. Israel has the right, they believe, to live securely within expanded borders of the Jewish state. In their view God has granted sovereignty to his people to rule exclusively over the land that was promised to the patriarchs. Many of these Christian believers are convinced that there will eventually be an apocalyptic war between God and evil in the near future: as a consequence, there can be no peace between Jews and Arabs.

What is crucial for us to note is that this pessimistic eschatology is based on biblical prophecy. Contemporary Christian Zionism is based on the Hebrew scriptures. This, it seems to me, is profoundly misguided and highly dangerous. The contributors to this book are attempting to illuminate the connection between sacred texts and political affairs. What I have attempted to show is how the conflict in the Middle East is fuelled in part by a fundamentalist reading of the Hebrew Bible. For the evangelical Christians I have discussed, there can be no compromise with the Palestinian people. God's providential plan is unfolding before our eyes. To escape the coming days of Tribulation, born-again Christians must embrace Christ in the hope that they will be 'raptured'. As you might expect, critics of Christian Zionism have been vociferous in their denunciation of such a world view. In the media Christian Zionists are often portrayed as dangerous and deluded. Thus the British commentator Robert Fisk charged in a column in the *Independent* that President George Bush had legitimized terrorism by

> giving way to the crazed world of Christian Zionism. The fundamentalist Christians, who support Israel's theft of the West Bank on the grounds that the state of Israel must exist there according to God's law until the Second Coming,

believe that Jesus will return to earth and the Israelis . . . will then have to convert to Christianity or die in the Battle of Armageddon.[6]

A range of popularized books dealing with Christian Zionism have followed a similar line. In her study of Christian Zionism, *Prophecy and Politics*,[7] for example, Grace Halsell argues that Christian Zionists practise the same form of muscular Christianity that their forefathers once followed when they slaughtered Indians to win the West. The American fundamentalists, she claims, see Armageddon as an event most earnestly to be desired. In the Arab world, the Palestinian scholar Edward Said stated in the Egyptian weekly *Al-Ahram* that

> the vast number of Christian fanatics in the US, who form the core of George Bush's support . . . are, in my opinion, a menace to the world and furnish Bush's government with its rationale for punishing evil while righteously condemning whole populations to submission and poverty.

In his view, the Christian right is rabidly pro-Israel and deeply anti-Semitic for believing that Jews who do not convert at the Messiah's coming will be doomed to perdition.[8]

Alongside such criticism, a number of Christian scholars have been anxious to illustrate that Christian Zionism does not correspond to traditional Christian teaching. Pre-eminent among such writers, Stephen Sizer in *Christian Zionism: Road Map to Armageddon* outlines a number of objections to its central characteristics:

1 A literalist and futurist reading of prophecy is the foundation upon which the other six tenets are based. However . . . this method of interpretation is no more consistent or free of presuppositional influence than

any other, and is at times inconsistent, contradictory and arbitrary.

2 A belief that the Jews remain God's chosen people, and separate from the church, flows from this literalist hermeneutic. While covenantal and dispensational Christian Zionists view the relationship between the church and Israel somewhat differently, the consequences of both are essentially the same: Israel is elevated to a status above the church; for dispensationalists at least, Israel will replace the church on earth; while Christians, and indeed whole nations, will be blessed through their association with, and support of, Israel. This view is entirely at variance with the New Testament which universalizes the concept of the people of God and makes chosenness conditional on faith in Jesus Christ.

3 Belief in a final restoration of the Jews to Zion is also based on a literal and futurist reading of selective Old Testament prophecies. However, the texts themselves indicate that such a return occurred under Ezra and Nehemiah and that no further return is to be anticipated. It may be argued that Jesus repudiated any such expectation. New Testament writers apply such Old Testament promises to both believing Jews and Gentiles.

4 It is also an article of faith that Eretz or greater Israel, extending from the River of Egypt to the Euphrates, is the Jewish inheritance originally promised unconditionally to Abraham and his descendants for ever.

5 Jerusalem, or Zion, lies at the heart of Christian Zionism. The city is seen as the eternal, undivided and exclusive Jewish capital. Nothing in the New Testament, however, substantiates this claim. Instead Christians are called to break with any dependency upon an earthly city and by faith to recognize that they are already citizens of the heavenly Jerusalem.

6 Most controversially, many believe the temple must be rebuilt and sacrifices re-instituted in order that it can be desecrated by the Antichrist before Jesus returns. The New Testament is emphatic that, after the death of Christ, the temple, priestly caste and sacrificial system became obsolete and their perpetuation apostate.

7 For virtually all Christian Zionists, the immediate future is intrinsically pessimistic. The battle of Armageddon will, they claim, lead to the death of two-thirds of the Jewish people before Christ returns to save a remnant. He will judge the world on the basis of how the nations have treated the Jews . . . Christian Zionism's particular reading of history and contemporary events, sustained by the dubious exegesis of selective biblical texts, sets Israel and the Jewish people apart from other peoples in the Middle East. In so doing, however, unintentionally, it justifies the endemic racism intrinsic to Zionism, exacerbates tensions between Jews and Palestinians and undermines attempts to find a peaceful resolution to the Palestinian-Israeli conflict.[9]

Use of the Bible by ultra-Orthodox Jewish Zionists

So far we have been looking at the impact of Christian Zionism on Middle East affairs. I want now to turn our attention to parallel developments in Judaism. Like Christian Zionists, ultra-Orthodox Jewish Zionists have promoted an aggressive policy of expansion in the Holy Land based on biblical teaching. Pre-eminent among these Jewish fundamentalists is the messianic movement *Gush Emunim* ('the block of the faithful'). From the outset, it adopted an extremist style of political action. The spiritual inspiration for this movement came directly out of the events of the Six-Day War of 1967. Israel's victory brought about the reunification of Jerusalem, the return to Israel of biblical Judaea and Samaria (the West Bank), the conquest of Sinai and the takeover of the Golan Heights.

In the view of a number of Orthodox Jews, these events were a miracle. The God of Israel had once again showed his strength. He came to rescue his people in their worst moment of fear. In one blow he had restored all of Eretz Yisrael. In the view of Rabbi Zvi Yehuda Kook, who had succeeded his father Rabbi Avraham Yitzhak ha-Cohen Kook as head of the Yeshivat Merkaz ha-Rav in Jerusalem, the Six-Day War marked the beginning of the messianic age. His disciples became missionaries with unshakeable confidence in the teaching of their leader. According to Kook, the entire historic land of Israel must be annexed to the State of Israel in anticipation of the arrival of the Messiah.

The founding meeting of *Gush Emunim* took place in March 1974 at Kfar Etzion, a West Bank kibbutz that had been seized by the Arabs in the War of Independence and recovered by Israel in the Six-Day War. At that time, the organization was declared to be a faction within the National Religious Party (NRP). After a short period of NRP existence, *Gush Emunim* left the party, and ever since it has refused to identify with any Israeli political party. From the beginning most of its members have been yeshivah graduates,[10] rabbis and teachers who were opposed to any form of territorial concession and were determined to promote Jewish settlement in the Occupied Territories.

During the Rabin government (1974–77), *Gush Emunim* operated in three spheres: it organized protests and demonstrations against the interim agreements with Egypt and Syria and against political and diplomatic activity related to these agreements; it promoted activities in Judaea and Samaria to highlight the Jewish attachment to these parts of Eretz Yisrael; and it carried out settlement operations in the Occupied Territories. Attention-focusing activities by *Gush Emunim* to stress Jewish attachment to Judaea and Samaria began with 'Operation Go-Around', which took place in October 1974. In December 1975 supporters of the movement spread out across mountaintops in Judaea and Samaria in a candle-lighting operation. During the Passover holiday in 1976 a tradition began of hiking across Samaria. Among those who participated in this event was Menachem Begin, the future Prime Minister of Israel.

The Likud victory in May 1977 encouraged the leaders of the movement to believe that their cause was gaining official support. Nonetheless, the Camp David accords, the Autonomy Plan and the government's commitment to give up the Rafiah Salient caused considerable concern. Determined to subvert concessions to Palestinian demands, a new group including members from *Gush Emunim* was formed – 'The Covenant of the Eretz Israel Faithful' – which declared war on the Camp David accords. Subsequently, the whole group founded the Tehiya movement. During this period key activists in *Gush Emunim* became ardent settlers. The ideology of *Gush Emunim* is based on the theology of Rabbi Avraham Kook, the former chief rabbi of Israel and father of Rabbi Zvi Yehuda Kook. According to Kook, the redemption has begun. With the rise of modern Zionism, the political gains of the Zionist movement, the Balfour Declaration, and the Zionist enterprise, God's providential plan for the Jewish people is unfolding. Basing his views on the kabbalah (Jewish mystical texts) Kook argued that what we experience in our daily life is in fact an unveiling of God's hand in history. God has his own way of bringing about redemption, he argued, even if those who play a messianic role in history (secular Jews) are not fully aware of God's providential plan.

In light of Kook's teaching, the Six-Day War in which Judaea and Samaria were conquered was an expression of the messianic process that began with the birth of modern Zionism. In this context, the land of Israel and the Jewish people are inextricably linked. According to this view, the complete land of Israel is not limited to the post-1967 borders but comprises the historic land of Israel of the covenant as described in scripture. Thus the settlements of *Gush Emunim* are more than a means of taking over the land of Judaea and Samaria; rather, they represent the unfolding of God's providential will. In this light, the Palestinian quest for self-determination is meaningless. The Arab demands are immoral since they conflict with God's plan for his chosen people. The practical implication of this position is that the Arabs who live within the Green Line or in Judaea and Samaria should be presented with three alternatives: (1) to acknowledge the legitimacy of the Zionist doctrine and receive full rights, including the right to elect and be elected to the Knesset (the Israeli parliament); (2) to obey the lands of the state without formal recognition of Zionism, and in return be granted full rights of resident aliens; or (3) be offered economic incentives to emigrate to Arab countries.

Alongside the creation of *Gush Emunim*, an underground movement comprised of several members of *Gush Emunim*, undertook to challenge the Islamic presence on the Temple Mount. According to these activists, the Muslim Dome of the Rock was an abomination and they resolved to destroy it. This plan was initiated by Yeshua Ben Shoshan and Yehuda Etzion who were closely affiliated with *Gush Emunim* and its settlement drive. In their view, the Camp David accords had a theological cause. It was a direct signal from heaven that a major national offence was committed, a sin that was responsible for political disaster and its consequences. Only one act of desecration could match the magnitude of the setback: the presence of Muslims and their shrine on the Temple Mount.

In early 1980 a secret meeting was convened by Yehuda Etzion and Menachem Livni. The main speaker was Yehuda Etzion, who presented a redemption theology based on the writings of the ultranationalist thinker Shabtai Ben Dov. The removal of the Muslim mosques, he argued, would spark a new light in the nation and trigger a major spiritual revolution. Menachem Livni, a Hebron engineer, agreed with Etzion but was apprehensive about the consequences. Livni's conclusion, which was accepted by the group, was that concrete preparations for blowing up the Dome of the Rook should start immediately. In May a group of yeshivah students were fired on by Arabs, resulting in six deaths. In response, Menahem Livni and Yehuda Etzion launched an assault on five Arab leaders. Subsequently the group resumed preparations for blowing up the Dome of the Rock. Yet, despite such determination, the attack was never carried out.

Other Israeli groups conceived other schemes. In the 1980s the 'Temple Mount' and 'Land of Israel Faithful' were founded by Gershon Salomon, a soldier who had helped liberate the Temple Mount during the Six-Day War. Critical of Moshe Dayan, who had returned control of the Temple Mount to Muslims, Salomon and his followers were determined to seize control. Anxious to achieve this end, Salomon sought the support of American dispensationalists, who viewed him as a pious Jew who believed that God's plan for his people in the last days required the construction of the Temple on the Temple Mount in anticipation of Jesus' return. During the 1990s Salomon lectured to evangelical tour groups to Israel and raised money from American evangelists.

Another important Jewish figure on the dispensationalist scheme was Stanley Goldfoot, a South African immigrant to Israel, who was connected to the Stern Gang and played a major role in the 1946 bombing of the King David Hotel and the murder of the UN Middle East emissary, Count Bernadotte. In the 1980s he and various dispensationalists founded the 'Jerusalem Temple Movement' in Israel. Anxious to locate the original Temple site, Goldfoot encouraged Lambert Dolphin, a dispensationalist and physicist at Stanford Research Institute in California, to use an x-ray system to conduct tests on the Temple Mount. In 1983 Dolphin and his crew attempted to investigate the Temple Mount but were stopped by the police. Another right-wing Israeli group that has drawn on dispensationalist support is the Temple Institute founded in 1986 by Rabbi Yisrael Ariel. Its aim is to educate Israelis about the significance of the Third Temple and to prepare for its creation. A veteran of the liberation of the Temple Mount during the Six-Day War, Ariel believes that Israel's future depends on rebuilding the Temple. When this is achieved, God's original promises to Abraham will be fulfilled, including Israel's possession of the territories promised to Abraham's descendants.

In certain respects these ultra-Orthodox Jews share the same religious agenda as Christian Zionists. As the influential critic of Christian Zionism, Stephen Sizer, remarked:

> Whether consciously or otherwise, Christian Zionists subscribe to a religious agenda best expressed by Rabbi Shlomo Aviner, who claims: 'We should not forget ... that the supreme purpose of the ingathering of exiles and the

establishment of our State is the building of the Temple. The Temple is at the very top of the pyramid.' Another rabbi, Yisrael Meida, explains the link between politics and theology within Jewish Zionism: 'It is all a matter of sovereignty. He who controls the Temple Mount, controls Jerusalem. And he who controls Jerusalem, controls the land of Israel.' This paradigm may be illustrated by way of three concentric rings. The land represents the middle ring and the Temple is the central ring. The three rings comprise the Zionist agenda by which the Land was claimed in 1948, the Old City of Jerusalem was occupied in 1967 and the Temple site is being contested. For the religious Zionist, Jewish or Christian, the three are inextricably linked.[11]

In my view, it would be far better to set aside the quest to draw inspiration from the Bible to solve the problems of the Middle East. The example of the Christian Zionists and of Orthodox extremists illustrates the dangers of the selective use of biblical texts. Instead of providing a bridge between Jews and Muslims, the Bible has become an obstacle to peace. This is the point made recently by Jonathan Kuttab, a Palestinian Christian in his reflections on the Middle East crisis:

> Palestinian Christians have suffered much at the hand of theologies and interpretations of scripture that provided a mantle of divine legitimisation to the ideology of Zionism and the political movement that worked for their displacement from their homeland, and built a Jewish state on the basis of their exile and oppression. One of our constant complaints was that Christian Zionism ignores our national rights. The creation of the state of Israel was done on our land and the ingathering of Jews from all the world came at the price of exiling and scattering our people throughout the world. All this was supported by Christian theologies that

ignored or delegitimized us as a people, claiming a divine imperative based on scripture for the creation of the state of Israel.[12]

These are strong words, and I cannot agree with this analysis of the creation of the Jewish state. Yet, Kuttab is right about the perils of interpreting world events in the light of scriptural teaching. Here I want to offer a plea: Let us take leave of the Bible. It will not help us to solve the overwhelming dilemmas of the Middle East crisis. Let us take leave of biblical prophecy in attempting to solve the problems that beset Arabs and Jews. Scripture is a hindrance. It is a snare and a delusion. What we need instead is good will, compassion and common sense.

Notes

1 Dale Crowley, quoted in Grace Halsell, *Forcing God's Hand: Why Millions Pray for a Quick Rapture and Destruction of Planet Earth* (Brentwood MD, Amana Publications, 2003), p. 5.
2 Jan Willem van der Hoeven, cited in Stephen Sizer, *Christian Zionism: Road Map to Armageddon?* (Leicester: InterVarsity Press, 2005), p. 243.
3 Hal Lindsey, cited in Sizer, *Christian Zionism*, p. 243.
4 Sizer, *Christian Zionism*, p. 248.
5 David Brickner, cited in Sizer, *Christian Zionism*, p. 250.
6 Robert Fisk, 'By endorsing Ariel Sharon's plan George Bush has legitimized terrorism', *Independent*, 16 April 2004.
7 Grace Halsell, *Prophesy and Politics: The Secret Alliance between Israel and the US Christian Right* (Independent Publishers Group, 1989).
8 David Parsons, 'Swords into Ploughshares' (Jerusalem: International Christian Embassy Jerusalem), p. 9.
9 Sizer, *Christian Zionism*, pp. 202–5.
10 Graduates of Orthodox schools for the study of the Hebrew scriptures.

11 Sizer, *Christian Zionism*, p. 21.
12 Jonathan Kuttab, 'An Open Letter to the Archbishop of Canterbury from a Palestinian Christian', 9 September 2004. http://www.christianzionism.org/articlesN.asp.

6

Religious traditions in the context of a liberal democracy

SHIRLEY WILLIAMS

I thought I might start with a little story which is sometimes told about the beginning of the world, and which seems appropriate. At the beginning of the world there was a discussion about who was really responsible for creation, between a doctor, a lawyer and a politician. The doctor said, 'Undoubtedly, I came first because I brought Eve out of Adam's rib.' The lawyer disagreed and said, 'No, I came first; I have priority because, after all, I brought order out of chaos.' And the politician just smiled and said, 'Who do you think brought the original chaos?' Now in this deep discussion the one person who stood outside it all was a theologian, and the reason that he or she stood outside it all was because he already knew the answer and did not deign to take part in the discussion.

We live in a country which is very, very different from the one in which I was brought up. I was involved in politics as a schoolgirl, then as a student in the 1950s, and could hardly wait to become an active member of Parliament in 1964. But the distinctions between that society and this one run very deep. The England of the 1950s – and I use the word England advisedly; I am well aware there are Scotland and Wales – was largely homogeneous in terms of race. It was still very structured in terms of class, with people, generally speaking, knowing that where they came from would determine where they went. It was also a society in which for a woman to run for Parliament was still thought to be very rare, and not just rare but, in some cases, bizarre, and in which, even then, there was still largely a single faith that dominated the discussion between faiths. The 1960s, 70s, 80s, 90s have altered that out of all recognition. We are today, evidently, a multicultural, multiracial, multifaith society. And for us the great challenge is whether we can make of that rich mixture a society that is more exciting, more vivacious, more inclusive, or one that decides to fall back into conflict, argument, prejudice and hate.

In May 2007 I spoke in Trafalgar Square at a demonstration that was organized particularly by the churches, not least by the Archbishop of Canterbury and the Cardinal Archbishop of Westminster. It was a demonstration to say that strangers should become citizens. The basis of it was to argue that those who had been migrants in this country for many years should be given the rights of citizenship so that they ceased, as they do today, to live in the shadows. 'Strangers into Citizens' – that was the cry. And it was rather like the breaking of the chain of debt in the developing world, which has united the churches and other faiths behind this objective and is, I think, a very good example of the way in which the faiths can become rightly and properly involved in the political process.

That, however, is not what I will write about here. Rather, I'd like to focus, first of all, on the remarkable development of what one might call the philosophy of human rights, both nationally and internationally. I'd like to consider how far the international community has the duty to intervene in cases where states abuse their own citizens, or even go further, as in the case of ethnic cleansing in Kosovo and

Yugoslavia, genocide in Cambodia, in Srebrenica or in Rwanda – instances of the massacre of particular minorities or groups that are no longer in power in the state concerned. We have taken on, as an international society, the concept of 'crimes against humanity' and the concept of international human rights. But although we now call some of these things crimes against humanity, the international criminal justice system is extremely weak. It is weak partly because the laws that are written through the United Nations, or other international forums, are often laws without any effective means of punishing those who transgress them. They are often more statements of a moral law than actual existences of constitutional law. Second, this whole movement (and my essay will go round in a circle and end where it begins) is also crippled by the selective abdication of certain countries from the entire process, of whom the most distinctive and the most powerful are the old contenders of the Cold War: Russia and the United States. One of the most profound discussions today revolves around the whole question of where there is a moral duty to intervene outside one's own borders and whether that is justified or not. I shall also consider the old Christian concept of the 'just war' and what relevance that has for us today in the conflict situations that we confront. In doing so I will go back to some of the earliest Christian teaching, to St Thomas Aquinas in the thirteenth century, who picked up from St Augustine's work in the fifth century, to try to produce a more modern version of the concept of the just war.

Human rights in the Abrahamic religions

Let me begin, however, in a different place. It is, I think, important to observe that the three Abrahamic religions –

Judaism, Christianity and Islam – base respect for the human being on the belief that he or she is created in the image of God. They share, too, a sense of community held together by the duty to love one another, or at least to behave as if one loves one another. That may be the most that can be asked of us. All three Abrahamic religions recognize the obligation to welcome the stranger in our midst and to care for him or her as the Samaritan did in the biblical parable. I visited the exhibition called 'Sacred' at the British Library. It is a brilliant collection of the sacred texts and volumes and, in some cases, sacred artefacts of the Abrahamic religions. It brings out the extent to which, both in artistic beauty and also in the themes they are trying to get across, there is a very great deal in common. Let me just quote very briefly from three of the texts and you will notice, as I have done, how remarkably much in common there is between them.

The first is from Leviticus, much respected and admired in the Jewish faith: 'Thou shalt not avenge nor bear any grudge against the children of thy people but thou shalt love thy neighbour as thyself.' Much older, of course, than the New Testament. From the New Testament, that statement by the prophet is echoed: 'You shall love the Lord your God with all your heart, with all your soul, with all your mind. This is the great and first commandment. And a second is like it: you shall love your neighbour as yourself. On these two commandments depend all the Law and the Prophets' (Matthew 22.37–40). And then from a great Islamic Hadith: 'Allah is with all those who do good.' Echoes here from the Qur'an of what appears often, too, in the Bible. And then, I think in some ways the most meaningful for this topic, St Paul to the Galatians: 'There is neither Jew nor Greek, there is neither slave nor free, there is no male or female, for we are all one in Christ Jesus' (3.28).

The tradition and value of liberal democracy

Having reflected on the commonality of those great texts of the three Abrahamic faiths, let me now set the other side of the equation in my title; that is to say, what is the tradition and the value of liberal democracy? I will define the core principles of liberal democracy which go back, of course, much longer than the creation of my particular party, the Liberal Democrats, certainly back a couple of centuries, as being three. There are many we could add but these three are abiding and last over different centuries and decades and are not, therefore, simply reflective of the politics of the day. The first of them is a passionate commitment to individual liberty. The state, in the view of the liberal democratic tradition, must have a very powerful case indeed to limit individual liberty. It may do so because it has to on the grounds of having to protect its citizens, which is constitutionally the fundamental obligation of any state. But what is absolutely essential is that it should never, ever limit individual liberty beyond what is necessary for this purpose. I have to say that in the war on terror, as it is inappropriately called, there have been many occasions when that border has been crossed, I think, unnecessarily for the purpose of securing the safety of the citizens of the different countries that are involved in that ill-named war. Why 'ill-named war'? Because, essentially, terrorism should fall into the category of a crime against humanity rather than a war, which always suggests one nation against another. Terrorism is something that afflicts many nations. We recall the long history of the terrorism that occurred in Ireland, not only on the Sinn Fein side but also on the Loyalist side. We remember the terrorism that is still defacing Spain. We remember the terrorism that has raged in many parts of Asia. Terrorism is not a phenomenon related entirely to the al-Qaeda movement nor, for that matter, limited to the faith of Islam and nobody else. It is a universal rejection of the concept of the value of the individual and it does not matter whether the terrorist is a so-called Christian, so-called Muslim, so-called Jew or so-called anything else: what he or she is perpetrating is a crime against humanity. In my view, and I feel this very strongly, if we had recognized from the beginning that we were talking not about war, reflecting the battles of the Westphalian nation-states, but about crime, we would have united our people much more effectively against it because we would not have divided them by talking in terms of an old-fashioned and inappropriate concept.

The second commitment of liberal democrats is a commitment to social justice (which is not a focus in this essay). I use the words social justice essentially as a political expression of loving our neighbour. If you go out canvassing our voters, people will be a bit surprised if you appear on the doorstep saying, 'I am asking you to vote for me to show that you love your neighbour.' They might not understand quite what you were saying. But if you say, 'I am asking you to vote for me because my Party stands for social justice', that is much more widely understood and has, of course, a long history going back to Methodism and before that to many other Christian sources.

The third commitment has to do with the issue of international responsibility. And by 'international responsibility', what liberal democrats mean is the building of a world of law and justice which, hopefully, will eventually bring peace. People often talk about law and justice, but let me add one other dimension to that statement, and that is the dimension that we often forget, of truth and reconciliation and of forgiveness – great faith concepts that play an increasingly important part in a world riven by conflict. What we have discovered, amazingly, in recent years, is that conflicts are much more often put behind us by reconciliation and forgiveness than by the continuation of war. And when sometimes people speak with great pessimism about politics, I feel the need to remind them that politics also has its miracles, and to remind them of just three in recent years. The first of those miracles was the collapse of the Soviet Union without the loss, as far as I know, of a single human being. The second was the ending of apartheid in South Africa with the loss of only two human beings. And the third was the most recent, the final conclusion of the endless conflict, going back centuries as you know, in Northern Ireland, which has been a terrible advertisement for what Christians are supposed to believe – the brotherhood of man, the love of neighbour for neighbour. One has to thank God that that has come to an end, and to repeat: there are miracles in politics, and sometimes conflicts we think are totally unable to be resolved are, in fact, resolved by the coming together of human beings who recognize the need to forgive one another and to be reconciled.

The history of the doctrine of human rights

Let me go from that back to the doctrine of human rights and remind you briefly of its history. We can go right back to Genesis – 'Let us make man in our image, after our likeness' – the concept of the common divinity of human beings. We can also go back in a different line, a secular line, to Aristotle, and his explanation of the political rights of the citizens of Athens. That assumption, or concept, of natural rights which appears in an early form in Aristotle's politics has also, of course, very much affected the Anglo-Saxon tradition of human rights, which has not very often been expressed in law but more often in tradition and precedent. The major voice advocating natural rights – and do not miss the distinction between natural rights and human rights, though they are closely related – was, of course, that great seventeenth-century figure, John Locke, in his *Two Treatises of Government* of 1688. John Locke held that all men and women are born free and rational, equal in their fundamental entitlements and in the duties they owe to God and to society. In his view, they must judge how God, who created them, required them to live. This natural law can be understood through the exercise of a human being's divinely given reason. Now do not miss the nuance in what Locke had to say in what was the beginning of the Age of Enlightenment. What he had to say was that human beings had rights but they also had duties and obligations. In the human rights field it is quite often the case that we forget the duties and the obligations in our concentration on the rights. They are indissolubly linked together. Locke's work a century later inspired the American Revolution and you will all be familiar with this quotation: 'We hold these truths to be self-evident, that all men are created equal, that they are endowed by their Creator with certain unalienable rights and that among these are life, liberty and the pursuit of happiness.' You will see that this echoes Locke to a very great extent but does not mention obligations and duties.

The highest point reached by the human rights movement in the period after the Second World War came in 1948 with the Universal Declaration of Human Rights, which owed a very great deal to the tremendous efforts of Eleanor Roosevelt, the wife of Franklin Roosevelt – within her own right a remarkable woman. The United States in those days was a major champion of the cause of human rights, of international human rights, driven, I think, largely by the horrors of Fascism and the unspeakable awfulness of the Holocaust. Remembering those two things, what the Fascists had done and the specific existence or happening of the Holocaust, drove many of the politicians of the immediate post-World War Two world towards radical positions with regard to international law, human rights, and economic development, as was exemplified by the Marshall Plan. It was a heroic period of politics and we have not seen anything like it since. The passage of the Declaration of Human Rights reflected the earlier meeting at Dumbarton Oaks in 1944 when the United Nations was itself established. It is very interesting that in the agenda for that founding meeting of the United Nations, no reference whatsoever was made to human rights. But a small group of people who were helping to draft the United Nations' constitution insisted upon adding eight weighty words to what was described as the secondary duty and purpose of the United Nations. Those eight words were to 'promote respect for human rights and fundamental freedom'. Not many words, but they have been the platform upon which virtually the whole of the human rights movement has been built.

In respect of the Charter itself, there was just one provision which dealt with the difficulty of how you enforce human rights against a government that has no feeling for it; that is article seven of the United Nations Charter, under which the Security Council can deal with threats to peace or acts of aggression, if necessary by military intervention. It has to carry the support of the United Nations Security Council on which, as we all know, no fewer than five countries have a veto. It is important to remember that, because that veto has been wielded in certain cases precisely to prevent any intervention in an issue involving crimes against humanity. Before I get there, though, let me mention one other major problem about the doctrine of human rights which, in some ways, has become today a secular religion. It is very striking how human rights, paralleling the faith principles that I have described and quoted from – paralleling but not the same – has itself become a kind of secular religion particularly among educated and better-off peoples over the face of the globe.

The problem about human rights is that, so often, it is interpreted selectively. We support human rights except for those for whom we do not support it. Let me give you three examples. The first of those examples is slavery. We have recently been celebrating the abolition of slavery in Great Britain in 1807. We have been noticing that this is the second centenary anniversary of that abolition. We are proud of William Wilberforce and what he achieved. We completely forget that long before William Wilberforce there were already Christian voices raised against slavery. I will give you two very early examples. In 1435, Pope Eugene IV condemned the seizing of people on the Canary Islands for slavery and ordered those engaged in the trade, and I quote his words, 'to restore to their earlier liberty all and each person of either sex on pain of excommunication'. Two centuries after that, in 1686, the Holy Office of the Vatican condemned the abuses of slavery – in particular permanent slavery – as distinct from, for example, putting prisoners of war to work. Yet a century after that Thomas Jefferson, one of the Founding Fathers, was a slave owner who saw nothing wrong in that. Passionate though his commitment was to human rights, he did not see slaves as fully human and therefore human rights did not apply to them.

Of course, many of us know, there was a much bigger section of the population to whom human rights did not apply.

Women have been excluded from human rights for most of history, only being included in the franchise of democratic societies in the first half of the twentieth century. Soon after the French revolutionaries drew up the Declaration of the Rights of Man and of the Citizen in 1789, women involved in the revolution marched on Versailles to ask for a declaration on the rights of women. They said this:

> Having cut down a very large part of the forest of prejudices you would leave standing the oldest and most general of all abuses: the one which excludes [and forgive the eighteenth-century language] the most beautiful and the most loveable half of the inhabitants of this kingdom.

Their request was treated as ridiculous and turned down out of hand by the all-male revolutionary national assembly. But then that was nothing new.

The other group that has often been excluded from human rights, along with slaves and women, have been minorities from other races. We have seen over and over again that minorities from other races are treated differently than the host community, and often they are the objects of prejudice, discrimination and worse. Liberal democracy, picking up the other half of the equation, accepts, and is committed to, the universal application of human rights. It believes not only in declarations but in the international law that implements the principle. So Liberal Democrats strongly support the European Convention on Human Rights and the European court that enforces those rights. Incidentally, Europe is the only region in the world where an individual can bring his or her case before the court on the grounds that their rights have been abused by a state. Everywhere else, the state is protected and the individual can only bring a case against another individual, the state against another state.

Long ago in 1976, I recall that Roy Jenkins proposed to the Cabinet, of which, by then, I was a member, that we should incorporate the Convention on Human Rights into British law. We got three out of the twenty-odd members of the Cabinet to support us and it took until 1998 for a government to eventually accept the incorporation of that Convention, which finally came into force in 2000. It has already upheld the rights of pensioners; it has upheld the rights of mothers to flexible working; and it has upheld the right of people not to be sent to the United States to face capital punishment on a charge which is not accepted, ever, as leading to capital punishment within the European Union.

Just war and liberal interventionism

We come to the final part and, in some ways, the most difficult part, of this essay. And that is the subject of how far one can implement, as distinct from simply declaring, international human rights. We have had somewhat ineffective laws, we have had many wonderful declarations on the subject, and yet, if you look at the world, you will notice as I do that gross abuses of human rights still occur. Let me remind you only of the most recent ones. There was a massacre in cold blood of five thousand unarmed Muslim men and boys in Srebrenica in Bosnia-Herzegovina in 1995. The people who perpetrated that are still free and have never been brought to justice. There was the genocide in Cambodia of at least a million people or more which was only ended, as the world turned aside, by a military incursion by Vietnam in 1978, driven at least in part by the unstoppable flow of refugees from Cambodia with which it was unable to cope. There was ethnic cleansing in Kosovo in 1999, ended only by the military intervention of NATO and without United Nations legitimation, although retrospectively the United Nations did agree that the action against Kosovo was legitimate. Evidence was brought before the International Court at The Hague to show how far Mr Milošević had intended that there should be terrible vengeance exercised against the Albanian majority there. And of course, perhaps worst of all, there was the genocide in Rwanda which killed nearly a million people within three weeks and which the Canadian general appointed by the United Nations said could be stopped if he could be given only ten thousand troops. And the member states of the United Nations could not find between them ten thousand soldiers to go and support him in ending the massacre in Rwanda. Outraged by the ineffectiveness of the United Nations and, I think, one might say the unwillingness of its member states, and more generally of the international community, Tony Blair, in his famous speech on the doctrine of the international community given to the Chicago Economic Club on 24 April 1999, declared of the NATO intervention in Kosovo, 'No one in the West who has seen what is happening in Kosovo can doubt that NATO's military action is justified. This is a just war based not on territorial ambitions but on values. If we let an evil dictator range unchallenged we will have to spill infinitely more blood and treasure to stop him later.' I understand very well what drove Tony Blair at that point because I myself spent ten days in Kosovo with Paddy Ashdown looking at some of the things that were happening before there was any NATO intervention. And I still remember the terrible pain of seeing a child's sandal in the middle of a house that had been burned down.

This became known internationally as the doctrine of 'liberal interventionism', and it undoubtedly drove Mr Blair's foreign policy. The trouble was it was not consonant with the charter of the United Nations, which still accepts, with rare exceptions, the sanctity of national sovereignty. The efforts to reconcile human rights' doctrines with national sovereignty has more recently led to proposals for 'a duty to protect', an obligation on governments to protect their own citizens and to risk international intervention if those rights are abused by them. The initiator of the concept of the duty to protect, which has led to a long debate in United Nations' circles, was that splendid country Canada, which has consistently shown a huge amount of imaginative interest in the building of a world of international law. The chairman of the Committee on Intervention and State Sovereignty, which looked into this whole question, was Gareth Evans, the former foreign minister of Australia, and the present President of the International Crisis Group.

I think it is useful to test the doctrine of liberal interventionism, and there is an irony in that phrase, because as you well know, the Liberal Democrats did not support the war against Iraq, believing it would have to be legitimated by the United Nations to be accepted throughout the world as a legitimate action. Because the United Nations never agreed to legitimate that war we, as a Party, came out against it. But my point is a wider one. It is to make a quick comparison between the concept of a just war and the concept of liberal intervention.

Let us go back for a moment to the Christian doctors and thinkers of the Middle Ages and before. Aquinas, drawing on Augustine, in *Summa Theologica*, listed, in his own words, three specific requirements for a just war. These three specific requirements, he said, were first, and I quote his words, 'the authority of the sovereign by whose command the war is to be waged' – this is very significant. Second, 'a just cause is required, namely that those who are attacked should be attacked because they deserve it on account of some fault of their own'. Third, and this is very important and quite difficult, 'the belligerents should have a rightful intention intending the advancement of good and the avoidance of evil'. In fact, Augustine says, we do not seek peace in order to get war, but we go to war that we may have peace. Now test those conceptions (in a modern form they are slightly different and I will describe them in a moment) against the actual events we have seen over the last twenty years. First, proper authority. Aquinas almost certainly meant the king, a proper dynastic king, who would have had the authority, in his view, to be able to declare war. Today, as in the case of Iraq, we often mean the United Nations, which is the nearest we get to the proper authority in a global and globalizing world. Second, Aquinas said, there has to be a just cause. They must deserve it because of some wrongdoing, and this second reason is largely upheld in most of the cases we are looking at with two crying exceptions: the armed intervention into Cambodia and Laos, both of them neutral countries at the time of the American war in Vietnam, is very hard to put down as a just cause, although the countries were undoubtedly used by the Vietcong guerrillas. Both countries were neutral, neither country wished to be engaged in war, and therefore there are real questions about whether an attack on them could be brought within the bounds of the morality of the just war. In just war, force should be proportional; no use of unnecessary force. The view of the just war was very clear: you must never use more force than the minimum necessary to achieve your goal. And, of course, that depended upon the deep belief that you distinguish between soldiers and civilians, and you could not justify the killing of civilians except in very, very rare cases. That condition has been almost completely lost because of modern reliance on air power, particularly among the more sophisticated countries of the world, which simply means that proportionality has long since gone. As for Aquinas's third criterion, right intention: regime change is not a permissible reason under the United Nations Charter, and that therefore leaves huge questions about Iraq, Rwanda and Serbia.

Then I come to the last couple of criteria for a just war. Now these are fascinating. The first, showing, I think, the pragmatism of the Church, was that there must be a prospect of success. In Aquinas's day that just meant you were likely to win the war. Today it means something very different. It means that, in going to war, you must know how you are going to end it; you must have what is called in modern terms an 'exit strategy'. You must also know precisely how you are going to reconstruct and eventually make good the ruin that you have caused by embarking on a war at all. And on this one, as on proportionality, the modern world falls horribly short. We have certainly, in Iraq, but also in other cases which one can mention with other countries being involved, created a situation where we had little idea, indeed no plans, for reconstruction or for rehabilitation when we embarked upon the war. In my view that is one of the gravest charges that all of us have to face. Finally, is war a last resort? Well, to my certain knowledge, shortly before we went in and invaded Iraq, Hans Blix, the head of the inspection team for weapons of mass destruction, asked for just two more weeks to complete his work, at the end of which he could say, 'There are no weapons of mass destruction, to the best of my knowledge, in Iraq.' He could not say it until his task had been completed. Those two weeks were not granted to him. And in that we moved away from the concept of last resort, because it was not the last resort.

I regard the philosophy and the concept of the just war as a very, very important template against which to measure the justifiability of war. I am not, unlike my mother, a pacifist, but I am certainly somebody who believes that war should be only in the rarest cases used or necessary. I am not a pacifist because I could not in the end see any way to stop Hitler except by force. Maybe I was wrong. Maybe I had an inadequate belief in my fellow human beings' moral courage. To this day, I am not sure I was wrong. Most of the wars since the Second World War I have not regarded as justified, and I have not regarded them as being conducted as a last resort.

I mentioned miracles in politics, and to my mind one of the most exciting and, in some ways, miraculous developments of the last twenty or thirty years has been the gradual emergence of a whole philosophy about resolving conflict, about finding political and economic answers to what used to be the causes of war. For me, the European Union has been a staggering success in terms of uniting people who previously were fighting at every possible excuse. We cannot even think of war as a possibility on the continent of Europe, which now extends to Central and Eastern Europe as well as Western Europe. We British are astonishingly stingy in ever admitting anything that the European Union does is good, because what it has done is so big that we simply refuse to see it. The other element in this, a different one, is, of course, the slow emergence of the International Criminal Court which will be the final coping stone in the structure of a political cathedral, a cathedral dedicated to peace. We have not so far been able to carry what I referred to earlier as 'the abdicators' – the United States and Russia – into the

International Criminal Court. Both have so far refused to sign it or to ratify it. Almost the whole of the rest of the world, from Europe to Asia, has now come on board for an International Criminal Court, which, among other things, could try people responsible for crimes against humanity. I think this is one of the most exciting developments in recent history but it is, frankly, a race between conflict and peace, between faith in the ability of human beings to find peace and their natural, instinctive, ancient origins of evil.

Postscript

SEBASTIAN C. H. KIM AND JONATHAN DRAPER

The 2006–2007 Ebor Lectures, 'Liberating Texts? Revelation, Identity and Public Life' have coincided with an exhibition, called 'Sacred', of some of the finest texts from the Abrahamic religions, which showed at the British Library between April and September 2007. Visiting the exhibition gives a sense both of awe at the beauty and antiquity of the texts, and also of celebration at the diversity expressed within each of the three faiths. What makes these texts sacred is the inspiration they are in the life of each faith community. The exhibition demonstrated the relations of the texts to the worship, holy places, ceremonies and festivals of the communities. The exhibition made it clear that these sacred texts not only affect the 'religious' life of the communities, but also in most aspects, their daily life. The interpretation and application of these sacred texts in a wider context beyond their particular communities has been the subject of much discussion, especially in recent years.

The focus of the Ebor Lectures and of this book has been on this issue of the public relevance of sacred texts in the context of both the secular and the religious life of Britain and beyond. The contributors addressed the following questions: how can traditions of interpretation be used to release the potential of sacred texts for public life? How can sacred texts encourage respectful dialogue and conversation in a plural context? How can sacred texts be interpreted and performed in ways which illuminate and re-imagine public life? How do religious traditions negotiate their identity in relation to the meaning of their sacred texts in ways which are both faithful and open to new insight? How can a sacred text contribute to the exploration of public life – liberation, justice, truth, hope and identity? In other words, can religious texts which perform a vital function within a particular religious community, providing aspirations and insights for daily life, make sense to other religious communities and wider secular society? These questions are important in the endeavour to seek the public relevance of theology and also to the ongoing Ebor Lecture series.

At the Edict of Milan (313 CE) Christianity became a public religion, and gradually came to dominate the life of the people of Europe for centuries. However, the relationship between Christianity, the state and the public has not always been beneficial in the history of Europe. On the one hand, religion has inspired people's imaginations, piety and moral conduct, and has produced rich cultures and societies; on the other hand, religion has also triggered hatred and rejection of 'otherness' and, as a result, become a cause of some of the most dreadful conflicts and afflictions in human societies. Due to this negative legacy of history, and also as a consequence of secularism, modernity and the rise of fundamentalisms, in the context of the West in the twenty-first century, many people wish to restrict religion to the private area of life – it should be a private and personal matter, and faith communities should remain silent on public issues. In this complex situation religious communities often struggle to find an appropriate response. People prefer to use terms such as faith, spirituality (Paul Heelas and Linda Woodhead) or rite of passage (Kate Fox), instead of religion or theology. There is an alternative: for faith communities to take this situation as a challenge to show a spirit of integrity by actively engaging in the public sphere and collectively struggling with common problems faced today. In this process of the faith community regaining confidence, public theology does not try to possess the moral high ground nor arrogantly proclaim ready-made answers to problems, but takes the attitude of a fellow seeker for a common solution. Faith communities have rich resources to offer, and public theology wishes to channel the interactions between faith communities and the wider society.

In recent years, the idea of public theology has been articulated in various research centres in universities and seminaries around the world, and this has resulted in the formation of the Global Network for Public Theology and the launch of the *International Journal of Public Theology*. While individual scholars and centres are working on various projects and issues involving public theology, many of the discussions are devoted to the question of the rationale for the public involvement of theology, the appropriate methodology for it, and the question of which public issues theology must engage with. The scholars in this field reject not only the restriction of religion to the private sphere, but also Christian modernism and Christian fundamentalism. Instead, they assert the active involvement of theology in the public sphere because it is inherent in the nature of Christian theology.

Jürgen Moltmann asserts that theology must publicly maintain the universal concerns of God's coming kingdom because 'there is no Christian identity without public relevance, and no public relevance without theology's Christian identity', and 'as the theology of God's kingdom, theology has to be *public* theology' in the mode of 'public, critical and prophetic complaint to God – public, critical and prophetic hope in God'.[1] Though Moltmann's emphasis on the kingdom of God and his pioneering work of developing an authentic public or political theology is much appreciated, his insistence that the environment for this attempt should be theology faculties in university settings is rather limiting. Public theology is not purely an academic endeavour to be developed in academia and then conveyed to the wider public, but rather this type of theology has to be in interaction with churches, faith communities and wider society and, in turn, inform academia of its findings.

Discussing the methodology of theology in public, David Tracy carefully examines the three publics of theology: academy, church and society, and suggests that there are three types of theology corresponding respectively to each public: fundamental theology, systematic theology and practical theology. In particular, he regards practical theology as the appropriate method for dealing with the social, political and cultural issues in public life.[2] There is, however, a danger of isolating the three social realities, resulting in the lack of a comprehensive or coherent approach to issues that involve two or three types of public, such as the controversy in 2005–2006 about the cartoons of the Prophet Muhammad that created such dispute between Muslim communities and western media on the issues of freedom of expression and respect for faith.

The question becomes: how should we develop theological discourse which reflects the concerns of various publics – faith communities, academia and society – and also addresses the issues of contemporary society? Daniel Hardy's comment on the task of theology is helpful here:

The task of theology, then, is to begin from common practice and examine its quality in open trial by the use of natural reason in order to discover the truth of this practice, by a truth-directed reason; and the fulfilment of this purpose requires reference to the author of practice and practical reason. And the outcome of the trial should be an agreement on the proper organisation of common life which would actually promote the practice of society. It is notable that throughout the concern is public, theology mediated in public practice, the use of public reason, open trial of the truth and the achievement of truly social existence.[3]

It is indeed the task of any faith community to attend to the 'proper organization of common life' and to contribute to the betterment of wider society.

In our examination of sacred texts and public life, each of the contributors brought out significant implications for religious engagement in public life. John Sentamu speaks in a prophetic voice, discerning the purposes of God and challenging the churches and wider community on matters of justice and human dignity. David Ford encourages the academy to pursue wisdom alongside knowledge and learning. Ataullah Siddiqui urges religious and morally minded people of different persuasions to eschew fundamentalist attitudes and recognize the contexts from which their scriptures come. Frances Young's essay includes a plea for the creation of a truly pluralist society, pluralist because its diverse members participate with one another and so grow to understand each other. Dan Cohn-Sherbok encourages creativity in the nature of that engagement, pointing out that sometimes new ways need to be found to bring different groups together that avoid the old impasses. And Shirley Williams puts the application of religion to public life into practice by testing the decision to invade Iraq against the Christian theory of just war. The suggestions above are based on thorough and sound research, yet they are very practical, and we are grateful for their contributions.

The Ebor Lecture series is a small step towards making insights of faith communities available to the public sphere. In turn, it is our intention in making these lectures public, and in publishing them here, to invite the concerns and questions of a wider public to interact with religious approaches. It is our hope that the three publics – faith communities, academia and society – pursue together the common good in public life.

Notes

1 Jürgen Moltmann, *God for a Secular Society: The Public Relevance of Theology* (London: SCM Press, 1999), pp. 1–5.
2 David Tracy, *The Analogical Imagination: Christian Theology and the Culture of Pluralism* (London: SCM Press, 1981), pp. 56–7.
3 Daniel Hardy, 'Theology through Philosophy' in David Ford (ed.), *The Modern Theologians: An Introduction to Christian Theology in the Twentieth Century* (Oxford: Blackwell, 1989), vol. II, p. 33.

Index